BIRTH ANGELS

fulfilling your life purpose
with the 72 angels of
the kabbalah

TERAH COX

**Andrews McMeel
Publishing**

Kansas City

Library of Congress Cataloging-in-Publication Data
Cox, Terry.
    Birth angels : fulfilling your life purpose with the 72 angels of the kabbalah / Terah Cox.
        p. cm.
    Includes bibliographical references.
    ISBN: 0-7407-4171-3
        1. Cabala. 2. Angels—Miscellanea. 3. Birthdays—Miscellanea. 4. Birth, Hour of—Miscellanea. I. Title.
BF1623.C2C69 2004
135'.47—dc22   2003070888

04 05 06 07 08 MLT 10 9 8 7 6 5 4 3 2 1

Book design by Holly Camerlinck

Attention: Schools and Businesses
Andrews McMeel books are available at quantity discounts with bulk purchase for educational, business, or sales promotional use. For information, please write to: Special Sales Department, Andrews McMeel Publishing, 4520 Main Street, Kansas City, Missouri 64111.

If you want to know
what to be
in this life,
Look into the topmost sky
of your heart –
There you will find
a star worth reaching for . . .
There you will find a map
for the path of your feet . . .
For there, in your dreaming
heart of hearts,
quiver the folded wings of
an Angel who fell to Earth
to bring forth Heaven

— TERAH COX

CONTENTS

PREFACE

This book represents the first detailed introduction of the 72 Angels of the Kabbalistic Tree of Life to the English-speaking world. The difficult thing about writing it was determining how much to leave out. The multitraditioned and mystical influences that developed the system of the 72 Angels and the Tree of Life are deep and varied, with roots and branches in virtually every tradition on Earth. The more I researched through the centuries and contexts of influences, the more interconnected and interdependent I found them. Indeed, the differences among traditions often lie more in their cultural and linguistic context than in their core essence.

The system of the 72 Angels and the Tree of Life was developed by those who might have been called the "new age" Kabbalists of the Middle Ages. These spiritual pioneers—perhaps the earliest forerunners of the Renaissance—were mystics and scholars working within the Jewish Kabbalah (also *Cabala* or *Qabbala*) who were also involved with ancient alchemy, astrology, Neoplatonism, mystical and mainstream Christianity, Hinduism, Islam/Sufism, and other Eastern and native traditions. These Kabbalistic "rebels" sought to bring Divine mysteries to the everyday lives of both men and women, which was in direct opposition to the Judaic sanctions that forbade females or unmarried males under 40 to partake of any sacred or secret knowledge. Thus, spiritual practice with the 72 Angels and Tree of Life was not recognized by traditional Kabbalists. This, together with the suppression of all things non-Catholic by the Spanish Inquisition, kept the tradition hidden, and eventually unknown, until the 1975 excavation of a Jewish grotto in Gerona, Spain, by Spanish and French mystic explorers and scholars.

Elements of the tradition have been making their way to the United States over the last couple of years through European practitioners. In addition, there have been several books published that contain correspondences to the 72 Angels tradition. Two of these are *Angel Signs* by Albert Haldane and Simha Seraya, and *The 72 Names of God* by Yehudah Berg. The latter deals with the power of "scanning" the 72 three-letter combinations to access specific qualities of the Divine in order to change our lives. *Birth Angels* explores this concept through the intricately developed symbology of the Tree of Life and the Angelic Energies that embody the 72 three-letter sounds (see chapter 1). However much traditional theologies may take exception to these nontraditional presentations, their basic premises are in keeping with core elements of one of the most respected and earliest-known sacred texts, the *Sefer Yetzirah,* or Hebrew "Book of Creation."

I must note that, as it often occurs with mystical material, there are discrepancies in the meanings and date correspondences of the 72 Names, or Angels, among varied sources through the ages. *Birth Angels* uses the medieval system revealed by French writers Kabaleb and Haziel, who translated the twelfth- to fifteenth-century manuscripts discovered in Gerona, Spain. My own practical use of this system for a number of years, as well as that of several European teachers working within its depths, has shown uncanny viability of its correspondences to practitioners.

The modern discovery of the "individual-friendly" 72 Angels tradition couldn't be more timely in a world where so many organizations are suffering corruption and crises in their value systems. As Gregg Braden suggests in his recent groundbreaking book *The God Code,* if we are going to heal our organizations—and our earth—we must begin to heal the individuals who populate them. We have come to overidentify ourselves by our differences. We have lost sight of the samenesses of heart and soul that underlie our varieties of form and expression. Braden's remarkable research claims that not only are we all made of "God-stuff," but the ancient name of that which created us is actually imprinted as a decipherable code within the very DNA of each one of us, no matter what our race or culture. Along these lines, the 72 Angels reveal that we are composed of nameable qualities and substance of the Divine on every plane of our existence—physically, emotionally, mentally, and spiritually. Working with the 72 Angels enables us to know and name which "syllables" and particles of God-stuff each of us are composed of, as well as how to access and use them to fulfill the purposes of our particular humanity.

In deference to our differences of expression, I have chosen to use the term "Divine" throughout most of this book for the myriad names that different religions, cultures, and teachings use to describe what the Western world calls God, Creator, etc.

So often our concept of a thing is colored or limited by the way we experience it through the use or practice of others. The system of the 72 Angels appeals to me because it calls to the individual human heart. The 72 Angels offer us personal relationship and commingling with the Divine *so that we might know who we truly are, and thus come to know and partake consciously of That Which created us.* Ultimately, discovering our true identity—our uniqueness within the "All"—is our best chance of finding our true contributing place in the togetherness of our human family.

I do not offer this material as a master. Writers are often instructed to write what they know—I usually find myself writing about what I *want* to know. Thus, I offer this book as a student seeking to explore and share what I have received with the wells of other wisdom seekers. Feel free to take what you don't understand or agree with and translate it into your own vocabulary and context, or disregard it altogether. It seems that there are as many paths to the light as there are people seeking it, and the sincere heart is always met by inner and outer guides along the path the seeker chooses.

One of the magical things about inner work is that it is often guided and confirmed by external signs, circumstances, or encounters. And so, as synchronicity will have it, while I was writing this passage in a café one afternoon, two men approached and jokingly referred to themselves as Gabriel and Michael, saying they had a message from an old parable for me: "Take care when the wise man is pointing to the moon that you don't focus on his finger." This was perfectly timed to help me make this point. Words are pointers and catalysts to meaning, meant to guide our focus toward personal, and hopefully, illuminating experience. You don't need to read this or any other book to have the Angels in your life. They are already here. If you want to "activate" them, you must only invite them into your awareness. Speak the name of any Angel you would like to invoke. It will hear you and respond—in some sweet, gentle or crazy, subtle or loud, amazing but *always timely* way. The Angels *are* here with us. All we really need is the heart to receive them.

ACKNOWLEDGMENTS

This book came about through a series of remarkable encounters and collaborations that evolved from my work as a lyric writer in the music business. In 1996 I met a French-Canadian recording artist who changed his name and career direction from a successful pop career to begin recording songs of a more spiritual nature. I was referred to "Kaya" as a lyric collaborator for his project by New York songwriters Arnie Roman, Peter Zizzo, and Russ DeSalvo. During the time we worked together he related to me some of his experiences with the 72 Angels and how they had altered his life. Ultimately, Kaya met a Swiss-Canadian woman who taught the tradition in the same town in Quebec where they both lived. He introduced me to this woman, Christiane Muller, who eventually became his wife. Christiane is a walking light who has a wonderful ability to bring through the energies of the Angels during guided meditation and teaching. Eventually, I hosted several workshops in New York City and upstate New York for her where she began to work with the tradition in the United States.

I introduced my friends Carolyn and Tim Tenney to Kaya and Christiane, who subsequently hosted them in their home on occasion. When Carolyn and I experienced the uncanny power and practical applicability of the 72 Angels through these two remarkable teachers, we realized the need for a book to reveal the powerful scope of the tradition. Ultimately, Kaya and Christiane decided to write their own book in French,[1] and I continued to research and work with the 72 Angels in preparation to write a book in English. Carolyn, who brings the combined perspectives of Christianity and

---

[1] Excerpts from Kaya and Christiane's book-in-progress, *Les Ailes de la Vie*, which details their experiences with the 72 Angels personally and in their workshops, may be viewed on their website at www.72angels.ca.

the Siddha Yoga tradition, acted as my unofficial editor. Her spiritual and pragmatic insights helped to make this book a clearer, more accessible presentation of the 72 Angels and their wonderful ways of inhabiting and transforming every aspect of our lives.

I thank Christiane for introducing me to the French works by Haziel and Kabaleb, which reveal and expand on the 1975 discovery of early medieval materials on the 72 Angels tradition and the qualities of the Angels. Other works that contributed substantially to my understanding of elements surrounding the tradition were Kim Zetter's *Simple Kabbalah,* Jay Ramsay's *Alchemy,* Aryeh Kaplan's translation and commentary of the *Sefer Yetzirah,* Manley P. Hall's *Secret Teachings of All Ages,* Will Parfitt's *Living Qabalah,* Gregg Braden's *Isaiah Effect,* and the Prosveta Society's many transcribed lectures of Omraam Mikhaël Aïvanhov.

I also want to thank Dominic Petrillo for his graphics assistance on the early charts for the 72 Angels and the Tree of Life; Jodi Tomasso for her thoughtful questioning and input; Maryanne and Rich Syrek, Cecilia Durkin, and Greg Doyle for their early involvement and encouragement, James O'Connor for his artistic input, and Georgia Christy, Catherine Connick, and Marshall Mermell for the book loans. Personal thanks to all those who supported me in so many ways during my research and writing, especially Harriet and Ken Appleman, Libby Healy, Arnie and Tanya Roman, Hannah Campbell, Art, Stacy, Lindy and Sara Labriola, Betsy Thomas, Laurie Raphael, Eileen O'Hare, Teresa Peppard, Andrew Goldstein, Tina Shafer, Sara Etta, Paul Benson, Vanessa Hartlauer, Roseanne Hart, Christina Spangler, and Mia Tomic, my "angel-sent" assistant. A very special gratitude goes to my heartful and generous friends and compatriots Jane Gyulavary, Peg and Tom Clarkson, and Kathy Glass, who continue to hang out on some adventurous limbs with me.

Special acknowledgment goes to Rob Weisbach, publishing maven who understood the uniqueness of this project and served as my first advisor. A mountain of thanks goes to my agent, June

Clark, who worked creatively with me to refine the proposal that eventually secured a publishing contract. Thanks to Derek Meade for the introduction to June, and to Del Bryant for his referral to Derek. Lastly, thanks to editorial assistant Lillian Ruggles for her good-natured thoroughness, all the designers, copyeditors, and proofreaders who helped to preserve the feeling of the book, and to my publishing editor Patty Rice, a wonderful separator of wheat from chaff, who had the vision and commitment to break new ground with me. *It really does "take a village"!*

INTRODUCTION

The tradition of the 72 Angels and the Tree of Life expands, enlivens, and gives deep personal relevance to our age-old ideas of Angels. Representing actual embodiments of the 72 Names and Person of the Divine, each of the 72 Angelic Energies has a specific name, quality, and function, as well as particular days and times of governing. At every moment of every day there is a specific nameable "Presence" through which we may engage certain aspects and energies of the Divine to facilitate, strengthen, or heal corresponding aspects of ourselves. In the 72 Angels tradition elements of astrology and the concept of "Guardian Angels" take on more potency and personal relevance. The tradition states that we are each watched over and helped throughout our lives by three *nameable and invokable* Angelic Energies that correspond to our date and time of birth. By working with our "Birth Angels," along with the rest of the 72 Angels of the Tree of Life, we cultivate lifelong spiritual allies that can help us elevate and ennoble our human purposes and potentials.

The profound experiences of diverse mystics and spiritual masters throughout the ages seem to imply that "all roads lead home" for the willing heart. Whatever path a seeker chooses—there is he or she met by the Divine in a way and language that best speaks to that individual's cultural and experiential context. Although the 72 Angels tradition emerged through the mystical counterpart of Judaism known as the Kabbalah, its elements were systematized by mystics and scholars from many traditions. The core premise of the 72 Angels, like most mystical traditions, is based on the unquashable idea that every individual, if he or she so chooses, has the right to seek and commune with the Divine without interpreters and other go-betweens. The tradition of the 72 Angels suggests that our "salvation" is not the road we walk, the scenery we enjoy or endure, or the language and props we use—but rather the quality of heart that drives us on.

This tradition is a pathwork of the heart that provides a unique and practical way to access the Divine in our daily lives. Teachers and teachings manifest themselves throughout our lives "when the student is ready." The 72 Angels tradition came to me when I was working with my own path as a "spiritual nomad." I have long identified with the "way of the fool"—the way of "no way/all ways"— which partakes of all traditions but affiliates with none. The 72 Angels tradition contains all the spiritual and philosophical elements that had resonated with me from various traditions I had "visited" throughout my life. In addition, elements of the 72 Angels tradition inhabit the core principles of all traditions—from ancient to modern. Within the mystical counterparts of most religions, the kinetic principles of love both fulfill and take priority over dogma. Likewise, the 72 Angels empower us as individuals to seek, find, and ultimately embody the Divine through ongoing communion at the inner altars of our own hearts.

What I particularly like about the 72 Angels tradition is that it reveals *why* and *how* the human heart is so powerfully endowed. Furthermore, it gives us *practical ways* to continually access this power with personal relevance. Engaging our Birth Angels enables us to utilize and even increase the teaching signs, synchronicities, and wonders in our daily lives. By working with the specific aspects of the Divine that correspond to our own qualities, challenges, purposes, and potentials, we can become healed and "trued-up" so that we may more fully manifest ourselves on Earth.

I.

IN THE BEGINNING
origin, description, and purpose
of the 72 Angels

The origin of the 72 Angels tradition can be traced to the eleventh- to twelfth-century school of practical Kabbalah, the "Kahal," which was started by a forward-thinking French Kabbalist, Isaac the Blind, and his collaborators. From the twelfth to fifteenth centuries in Spain, France, and Italy, exploration and sharing of old and new ideas and discoveries among scholars and mystics was at a peak. The Kahal visionaries worked within the infinite depth of the Kabbalah (Jewish mysticism), while at the same time drawing upon its correspondences in Gnostic Christianity, Hermetics (alchemy), Sufism, the Tao, astrology, and Pythagorean and Neoplatonic principles. These multitraditioned medieval Kabbalists believed that individuals from all walks of life had the right to personally engage the Divine in their daily lives. They worked together for generations to free the sacred mysteries from the sanctions of Jewish law that forbade anyone but married males over 40 to partake of them.

The city of Gerona, Spain, ultimately became the international hub of the Kahal; however, during the 15th-century Spanish Inquisition the school was closed. The Jewish quarter in Gerona was walled in, and Kabbalah students and scholars were forced to either convert to Catholicism or flee. It was almost five centuries later, in 1975, when the quarter was finally excavated by a small group of citizens. A man whose family home had abutted the wall since it was built initiated the excavation. Inside, the medieval writings detailing the system and symbology of the Tree of Life and the 72 Angels were discovered. During the 1980s and 1990s two brothers translated and elaborated upon these and other related medieval manuscripts. The works of Haziel and Kabaleb were published in French by Editions Bussiere in Paris and ultimately made their way to Switzerland and French-speaking Quebec. Christiane Muller, originally from Switzerland, and her French-Canadian partner Kaya, are among the teachers and mystics who currently conduct ongoing workshops dealing with the 72 Angels tradition.

what the 72 Angels Are

Angels are commonly thought of us messengers and facilitators between the Divine/Heaven/above and the Human/Earth/below. The 72 Angels are the inhabitants of the Nine Angelic Choirs on the Tree of Life, and are what we often refer to as Guardian Angels, Divine Messengers, Emissaries of Light, Bestowers of Grace, and Bringers of Miracles. The twentieth-century "maverick" Kabbalist Omraam Mikhaël Aîvanhov described how the Angels connect us to the energies of the Divine by using the metaphor of the step-down transformer—an electrical device (the Angels) that decreases a high-voltage source (the Divine) so that it can be plugged into a lower voltage receptor (the human). Conversely, when we invoke, pray, or appeal to the Divine, the Angels serve as "amplifiers" to transmit our seemingly small and finite communication to the vast and infinite Divine.

Scholars and mystics from both Renaissance and medieval times provide a more intimate and detailed understanding of Angels than popular angelology. According to this tradition, *the 72 Angels are energetic embodiments and vibratory expressions of the 72 Names, Qualities, and Person of the Divine. They awaken our consciousness to the presence of the Divine already within us and by partaking of them, we activate aspects of the Divine within our own humanity.* Each Angelic Energy expresses a specific aspect of Divine (1) Manifestation/Will/Purpose, (2) Love, and (3) Intellect, which corresponds to the same qualities in humans. While we are said to contain the qualities of all 72 Angels in varying degrees, we have correspondences to particular Angelic Energies according to our date and time of birth, which are our personal "Birth Angels."

What's in a Name?

The names of the 72 Angels were discerned from the Bible's book of Exodus 14:19–21. Each verse contains 72 Hebrew letters, which yield 72 three-letter combinations when written from right to left, left to right, and so on.[1] When "Yah/iah" or "El" are added to the end of each combination, they compose the 72 Names of God. (Classical Hebrew did not include vowels, which were added later for clarification.) Collectively, the 72 Names are referred to in Hebrew as the *Shem Ha Mephorash*, meaning "the Name in Detail." The symbol representing this is the Tetragrammaton, a triangle containing the sacred four-lettered Name of God known as YHVH ("YeHoVaH" or "YaHWeH"), from which the 72 Names have derived. The letters in this sacred triangle are arranged so that the numerical sum of all the combinations of the four letters equals 72.[2]

---

[1] Malcolm Godwin's *Cabalistic Encyclopedia*, Llewellyn, 1999
[2] Manley P. Hall's *Secret Teachings of All Ages*, The Philosophical Research Society, 1988

The number 72 has numerous human correspondences. Below is a sampling from www.pages.globetrotter.net:

* The 72 races resulting from Noah
* The 70 ancients accompanying Moses that received an outpouring of the spirit, plus two others who had remained in the camp
* The 72 languages which resulted when speech was confused at the Tower of Babel
* The 72 disciples of Confucius, who died at the age of 72
* The two plus 70 disciples sent out by Jesus (Luke 9:57–62 and 10:1) to spread the Word
* The 72 years it takes for the axis of the earth to move one degree
* The mass of the Moon as 1/72 that of Earth
* The volume of Saturn as 72 times that of Earth
* The 72-hour life duration of the human egg
* The average of 72 cardiac pulsations per minute
* The 72 percent water that a human body is composed of
* The 72 joints of the body

The qualities of the Angels are determined partly by the numerical values and meanings of the Hebrew letters that compose their names. In Kabbalistic cosmology, the universe was created by 22 Divinely expulsed sounds. These 22 sounds, which are the 22 letters that make up the Hebrew alphabet, represented the first sparks of Divine Self-Expression. They are the means by which the One Divine Self manifested and multiplied Itself into the diverse forms of Creation via the Tree of Life. According to the *Sefer Yetzirah* ("Book of Creation," arguably attributed to Abraham), the earliest known Kabbalistic work about the formation of the Universe, each sound/Hebrew letter has a numerical value that corresponds to a particular quality of the Divine. Therefore, each sound, when expressed by the Divine, resulted in the creation of a particular form with both quantitative and qualitative elements of Itself.[3]

A growing number of works by scientists, mathematicians, and other scholars explores the uncanny and dynamic relationships between sounds, letters, numbers, and meaning. Gregg Braden's book *The God Code*, published in January 2004, is one of the most exciting. *The God Code* offers a remarkable body of scientific and scholarly research to "prove" some of our most profound spiritual truths through numerical and linguistic correspondences.

By translating the chemical and numerical equivalents of DNA into corresponding letters of the Hebrew alphabet, Braden and his experts have discovered what seems to be a text message in our cells, along with the "signature" of its author. The message is "God/Eternal Within Us," and the signature is the numerical equivalents of YHVH, the ancient name of the Divine. One of Braden's important resources in his search was the ancient *Sefer Yetzirah*, which revealed the secrets of creation via the 22 sounds and numerical qualities that became the Hebrew alphabet. This is the same cosmology that gave us the system of the 72 Angels and the Tree of Life. Thus, in keeping with the principles of the *Sepher Yetzirah*, each Hebrew letter that composes an Angel's name has a particular numerical association, conceptual meaning, and energetic quality. When we speak an Angel's name, we unleash within us the cumulative energetic charge held by the combined letters. This is why it is so powerful to speak the Angel's name, even as a mantra, during invocation or meditation.

---

[3] The Christian counterpart of this is known as the "Logos," which is referred to in the first chapter of the Bible's Book of John, "In the Beginning was the Word, the Word was with God . . . the Word was God . . . and the Word became Flesh." This concept of using sound (and thought) to create or alter reality has filtered through the ages into human spirituality, philosophy, and healing practices—from the multicultural religious and native traditions of chanting, singing, and drumming to the nineteenth- and twentieth-century proponents of "positive thinking" and the repetition of affirmations.

The Angelic Inhabitants of the Tree of Life

The 72 Angelic Energies are said to have originated and forever reside in the Tree of Life (see Appendix I). The Tree's 32 branches are composed of Ten Sephirot (spheres, or vessels, of Divine Energy that are numbered according to their order of emanation from the Divine) and the 22 Paths that connect them. The 72 Angels form the Nine Choirs of Angels that occupy each of Sephirot 1–9.[4] There are eight Angels in each choir, and each Angel carries out specific details of the qualities and functions of the Archangel that governs its corresponding Sephira. The Angels work with each other and their governing Archangels, as well as the other elements within the Tree, to implant on Earth a mirror image of what exists in the heavens.

In his book *Living Qabalah,* Will Parfitt suggests that we can work with the Tree either from the bottom up, representing the individual's ascent or return toward the spiritual, or from the top down, drawing spiritual energy into us from above. The Angels help us to "climb back up the Tree" and ascend in consciousness. They also bring Divine Energies "down" the Tree so that we might commune with, ingest, and assimilate the Divine within our humanity. In this way, we are lifted and ennobled in thought, speech, and action.

The Purpose of the 72 Angels on Earth

The 72 Angels help us "true-up" our lives. They remind us of where we came from and reconnect us to our Divine "power-source" so we may receive the bountiful, purposeful life intended for us. This is what it ultimately means to bring Heaven to Earth. The Angels transform our awareness so that we may recognize and embrace

---

[4] The Tenth Sephira is the Energy that manifested Earth and Mankind and represents the sphere of Saints and Beatified Souls.

the magnitude of ourselves. We are composed of all the Divine qualities that the Angels themselves embody. When we align with the Angelic Energies, we awaken and activate those qualities within us. In so doing, we increase our "image and likeness" to the Divine, which empowers us, paradoxically, to become more wholly human. *To be wholly human means to have all aspects of ourselves—physical, emotional, intellectual, and spiritual—working together in a state of equilibrium toward the fulfillment of our particular purposes, potentials, and dreams.*

The 72 Angels help us become what we are meant to be, and in fact who we already are behind the veil of our illusions and self-images. For a moment, put aside every self-limiting thought you have ever entertained and consider that it is we humans, in our unfolding uniquenesses, who enable the Divine to experience the utmost possibilities of Itself. Thus, it is not only our right—but also our sacred responsibility—to be, and to honor and enjoy all that we can while we are here on Earth.

2.

IN THE ARMS OF
OUR BIRTH ANGELS

working with our personal Divine guardians, "connectors," and consciousness-raisers

According to sacred mysteries, each one of us embodies the qualities of all 72 Angels as both realized and unrealized, or latent, potentials. The tradition takes on even more personal relevance through the three specific Angelic Energies that were in dominion at the exact time and day of our birth, and whose particular qualities correspond to our own. These are our "Birth Angels"—our personal internal guardians, helpers, and guides. Their purpose is to return us to awareness of the Divine—and its particular aspects within us—so that we might elevate our humanity, meet our challenges, and fulfill our unique purposes. Since our Birth Angels embody qualities similar to our own, when we invoke them we, in turn, are essentially invoking our own potential. Thus, the more we engage with our Birth Angels, the more full of our true selves we become.

Divine Blueprints

Our Birth Angels are the conveyors of a personal Divine "blueprint" for each of our lives. This blueprint is not meant to confine or determine us but rather to give us clues to the purposes our spirits have chosen, in collaboration with the Divine, for our earthly lives. The Angels are our perfect "mirror, mirror on the wall"! By seeing ourselves through their eyes, we can appreciate the uniqueness of ourselves and the special talents and gifts we possess. As we become more inhabited by the Angelic presences, our clarity and wholeness increase until we become reflections of the Angels themselves.

We are physical, emotional, intellectual, and spiritual beings. Therefore, each aspect of us is sacred and vital to our well-being and the full expression of our humanity. The Angels represent the Divine within our spirit component, which is expressed in our three other aspects. *Thus, each Angel has periods of influence when It corresponds to and helps us maximize particular qualities and functions in our physical/existential nature (**Incarnation Days**), our emotional nature (**Heart Days**), and our mental nature (**Intellect Time**).* As the Angels work with these levels of our own human qualities and functions, we are able to manifest corresponding levels of Divine Beingness and Expression in ways that are specific and supportive to each one of us.

The most powerful time to work with your Birth Angels is during their days and times of influence in the corresponding areas of your life.

1. An Angel's **Incarnation** dominion (plane of governing) corresponds to **one five-day period** in the 365- (or 366-) day year in which the Angel expresses particular qualities and functions of *Divine Manifestation, Will, and Purpose* on the human plane. *Thus, your **"Incarnation Angel"** corresponds to your **five-day period of birth** and particular qualities, functions, potentials, and challenges of your physical being, will, and purpose on Earth.* This is an Angel's strongest period of influence in your life.

2. An Angel's **Heart** dominion corresponds to **five separate days** in the 365-day year in which the Angel expresses particular qualities and functions of *Divine Love* on the human plane. *Thus, your "Heart Angel" corresponds to your **exact day of birth** and particular qualities, functions, potentials, and challenges of your emotions.* This is an Angel's second strongest period of influence. Since your Heart Angel governs four other one-day periods in the year, those days are also your Heart Angel days during which Its energies can be of particular help to your emotional well-being and growth.

3. An Angel's **Intellect** dominion corresponds to a **20-minute period** during the 24-hour day in which the Angel expresses particular qualities and functions of *Divine Intellect. Thus, your "Intellect Angel" corresponds to the **20-minute period of your birth** and particular qualities, functions, potentials, and challenges of your intellect, which includes your ability to grasp and apply Divine Principles and Truths in your life.* Those born at a cusp time, meaning on the hour or 20 minutes before or after (e.g., 11:00, 11:20, or 11:40) will have two Intellect Angels. This is an Angel's third most potent period of influence. Note that all 72 Angels have a particular 20-minute period during the 24-hour day in which they express Intellect influence—thus you could work with all three of your Birth Angels in any given day during their respective Intellect times.

Since an Angel's influence is strongest during its days and times of dominion, it is especially effective to work with them during those periods. An Angel's qualities will play out in us differently according to which period of dominion—Incarnation, Heart, or Intellect—that the Angel is expressing at any given time. For example, the primary quality/function of ARIEL, my Incarnation Angel, is "Perceiver and Revealer" of hidden or esoteric knowledge. The most potent time for me to tap into ARIEL's power to enhance my life purpose is the five-day period of my birth. However, when ARIEL is presiding in its one-day heart dominion (which occurs on five separate days each year), my life purpose to perceive and reveal may take on deepened potency if my heart/wisdom/emotions are more profoundly engaged on those days. This may also be a time to work on any emotional issues that may be distorting my perception or the way I reveal information to others. Likewise, when ARIEL is in its 20-minute period of Intellect dominion, my life purpose of perceiving and revealing may be heightened by a higher use of my mental faculties and the clearing of negative/inverted thought processes and attitudes.

When any one aspect of ourselves is debilitated, resistant, hurting, or frozen, our other aspects will eventually suffer. Since we are not a lump of unrelated parts, working with the Angels on all our levels enables us to evolve holistically. All our aspects are interconnected and interdependent within our internal and external human selves. Together they compose an ephemerally enlivened physical being that is more than the sum of our parts.

To "Know Thyself."

The Divine "mystery schools," which can be traced to the Egyptian and Greek times, have a primary mandate that was the first command of the Greek Oracle: "KNOW THYSELF." This was considered the holiest task an initiate must undertake, because by knowing the Self, one could ultimately come to know the Divine. This embraced the concept that the Human Self is a microcosm, or "miniworld," of the Divine macrocosm. We each contain the *essence* of the Divine, and we are each composed of a set of substances and qualities that constitute a particular *expression* of the Divine. Working with our Birth Angels helps answer the eternal questions of who we are and why we're here. If we are conscious of the Divine within us, we can discover the Divine blueprint for ourselves and our unique combination of physical, emotional, intellectual, and spiritual qualities. We can then make the best use of our talents and skills to accomplish our true purposes.

"Go" and "Return" Angels

With a few exceptions, each Angel has a "Go" or "Return" function on the Tree of Life that has to do with the directional flow of its Energies descending from the Divine down the Tree toward Humanity or ascending/returning up the Tree back toward the Divine. This also touches on the Kabbalistic and "alchemical"[1] premise that whatever we do on this earthly plane affects and alters the cosmic planes of existence as well.

The origin of this Go and Return ideology may be attributed partly to a passage in the *Sephirah Yetzirah* (Book of Creation) about the Ten Sephirot: ". . . the ten spheres [appear] out of Nothing . . . and they are without beginning or end. The Word of God is in them when they go forth and when they return." This relates to each Angel's dynamic within us. The "Go" Angels represent qualities we are meant to manifest externally—to the greater fullness of our *actions* and *expression* of Divine *Manifestation*. The "Return" Angels represent qualities we are meant to manifest internally—to accomplish the greater fullness of our *being*, which is ultimately a greater enrichment returned to the Divine *Beingness*. For example, if your Incarnation Angel is ASALIAH, a "return" Angel embodying "Contemplation," then the ability to be contemplative would *support* your external purpose rather than *become* your purpose; if Asaliah were a "go" Angel, you might have a propensity to become a religious contemplative.

Our internal and external aspects are meant to support and propel each other. Thus, each Angel has a Go or Return supporting Angel that helps to facilitate its (and our) qualities and functions. If we engage our Go and Return Angels we can deepen our effectiveness in working with our Birth Angels and round out the bigger picture of ourselves. These supporting Angels give our Birth

[1] From "alchemy," the ancient scientific and spiritual art of transformation concerned with turning base metal into gold and the base mettle of human substance into golden thoughts and deeds. See chapter 9 for elaboration.

Angels, and us, additional allies. They help us to understand which qualities we should internalize and which we should express more overtly. For example, my Incarnation Angel, ARIEL, is a "Go" Angel. This means that ARIEL's qualities/functions, as "Perceiver and Revealer" of esoteric knowledge, are manifested externally in my life purpose. This could, and does in my case, result in a career choice that utilizes these qualities. ARIEL's "Return Angel" is NANAEL, representing "Spiritual Communication," which indicates that ARIEL's outer purposes of perceiving and revealing will be supported and facilitated by spiritual communication—which also corresponds to my experience.

Since determining an Angel's Go or Return counterpart involves planetary aspects and can be somewhat complex, a list is provided in Appendix III of the Go and Return Angels for each of the 72 Angels.

The Astrology Angle

The qualities of the 72 Angels are determined not only by the numerical value and meanings of their names, but also by their astrological correspondences. The 72 Angels/"Aspects" of the Divine are said to have emanated through the 12 houses of the zodiac into the Ten Sephirotic vessels of the Tree of Life (see Appendix III). Each Angelic Energy is manifested through 5 degrees of the zodiac and governs *one five-day and five separate one-day periods in the 365/366-day year,*[2] *plus one 20-minute period in the 24-hour day.*[3] Thus, each Angel is associated with a particular planet and astrological sign which influence the way the Angel's qualities function on the human plane. In addition, since each Sephira is associated with a planetary aspect, the Angels residing within the Sephira are also affected by the Sephira's planet. When we give credence to astrology, we find that we may be subject to the same influences.

---

[2] 72x5=360 plus an overlapping of influence during five days to equal a 365-day year. (The extra day in our 366-day leap year is incorporated by the Angels that govern February 28.)
[3] 72x20=1440min÷60=24hrs.

Modern man has argued the efficacy of astrological influences *ad infinitum*, especially the questions and disparate views of free will and destiny. The ancients understood that the planetary heavens contained an energetic map, or template, for the procession of earthly cycles, conditions, and potentialities. By studying this map, an individual could find his or her place in the greater cosmological scheme. This could also serve as a guide for one's time and purpose on Earth and the ebb and flow of favorable astrological aspects and influences that can affect human cycles and conditions. One could also use this information as a portent of *possible* things to come, much in the way the three Magi (one of whom was said to be an astronomer/astrologer) followed the bright messianic star that appeared in the sky over Bethlehem to find the newborn Jesus. Seers and scientists alike took the earthly application of astronomy very seriously, and history is full of the importance attributed to their advice by royals and other government leaders, chieftains and military commanders. The machinations of Christianity, however—particularly from the time of the Spanish Inquisition—cast suspicion and heresy upon any influences that did not directly proceed from church authorities and interests.

In its highest application, astrology is not meant to be used for fortune-telling or supplanting human will. Rather, it offers us a forecast of favorable or unfavorable influences based on the energetic fields emitted by certain planetary and star configurations. Understood in this light, astrology can become a cosmic well of information to give more favorable timeliness and energy to our own choices and decisions.

Personally working with the 72 Angels has brought me closer to understanding how much every thing and being is interconnected, interdependent and influenced by every other thing and being. We are all part of the whole Divine and Human "cause and effect" relationship that the Tree of Life symbolizes. It plays out in every dynamic from the most minute to the most majestic, from the most intimate and personal to the most distant and objective.

Externally, we see it in the "ripple effect" from the simple act of throwing a stone into a pond, or the gravitational "agreement" that keeps the planets and stars from colliding into each other. When you consider that the Moon governs the tides of our oceans—and that the human body is 72 percent water—isn't it possible that we humans are also affected by the Moon?

Just as in the cosmic pattern, our human conditions, situations, and scenarios start with the action of "one" causal person, thing, or event that ultimately ripples out from the source many times. Each new "original cause" perpetuates a continuing cycle of effects and subsequent new causes. Working with the 72 Angels helps to purify and balance us internally, so that the effects we create on other things, people, and events become more and more light-and-life-affirming. As whole and productive individuals, we send ripples of energetic wholeness out to family, friends, and associates—as well as back up the Tree of Life to That Which originated and continues to sustain us.

3.

THE 72 ANGELS

The Angels' names, qualities,
and functions, sephira, astrological
associations, and periods of influence

Remember that your Birth Angels' qualities and functions represent those that are already present or in a potential state in your own life. In order for you to better relate with the Angels, their qualities are worded as ways in which they can be of influence or guidance to you as you invoke them. The three-step Angel path (see chapter 4) details how the Angels help to raise your awareness of their presence. This awareness facilitates their energies within you, helping you to become the best and fullest version of yourself as a unique spark of the Divine-on-Earth.

How to Read an Angel Chart

The key on the facing page will show you what each of the sections in an Angel chart correspond to. The following is a brief summary of the various components.

Angel's Number

Represents the Angel's order of emanation and descent from the Divine Oneness into its Sephirotic "residence" on the Tree of Life.

Angel's Name[1]

Represents a sound composed of three Hebrew letters (with vowels added by later scholars), which together express a particular quality and "energetic charge" of the Divine that is activated when we speak the Angel's name. The phonetic spelling provided indicates accented syllables in ALL CAPS. You will notice that all the names with two syllables have the accent on the last syllable (EL or IAH/YAH). Both of these syllables indicate that the Angel's name expresses a quality of God. Angel names with three or more syllables contain two accented syllables, one of which is always the last syllable.

Primary Quality

This is the primary Virtue/aspect/function of the Divine that the Angel particularly embodies and expresses. An Angel's qualities and functions on the human plane are determined by the combination of Hebrew letters that compose its name, its astrological associations, and its place (Sephira) on Tree of Life.

---

[1] There are discrepancies among various authors and systems as to the exact spellings of the names of the Angels and other elements of the Tree of Life. For the most part I have used the spellings used in the works of Kabaleb and Haziel, which draw from the materials on the tradition discovered in the 1975 excavation of the fifteenth-century Gerona grotto, as well as the works of other mystics and scholars of the time.

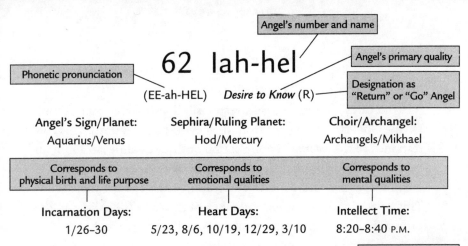

Angel's number and name

62 Iah-hel

Phonetic pronunciation

(EE-ah-HEL)   *Desire to Know* (R)

Angel's primary quality

Designation as "Return" or "Go" Angel

Angel's Sign/Planet:	Sephira/Ruling Planet:	Choir/Archangel:
Aquarius/Venus	Hod/Mercury	Archangels/Mikhael

Corresponds to physical birth and life purpose	Corresponds to emotional qualities	Corresponds to mental qualities
Incarnation Days:	Heart Days:	Intellect Time:
1/26–30	5/23, 8/6, 10/19, 12/29, 3/10	8:20–8:40 P.M.

VIRTUES

"Positive" qualities that Angel embodies, which correspond to our own qualities and potentials

▲ Encourages toward the road less traveled and productive disengagement from the material world in favor of adventures that bring knowledge

▲ Helps to understand the "world of creation" on the deepest and highest levels; helps to search for understanding of cause and effect in daily life and conditions

▲ Inspires the philosopher and mystic: helps guide the descent of knowledge from the mind into the heart, where knowledge is transformed into wisdom and understanding

▲ Fosters love of tranquility and solitude in order to facilitate receiving illumination and knowledge from within

▲ Helps to fulfill duties and obligations and to be distinguished by virtue and modesty

INVERSIONS

"Negative" manifestations of unused or ill-used virtues

▼ Tendency toward inconstancy, restlessness, and shallow uses of deeper subjects such as philosophy and spirituality

▼ Searches for luxury, pleasures; inconsequential use of time, associations, and communication

▼ Prone to unfaithfulness, disloyalties, scandals, rifts, and divorce between masculine and feminine

▼ Troubled, ill-at-ease, spiritually sick with many unresolvable problems

"G"/"R" /"S"—"Go," "Return," or "stable" Designation

"G" indicates that the Angel's responsibilities involve manifesting Divine Qualities (going out from the Divine into creation). This corresponds to the *external* manifestation of those qualities in a human being. "R" indicates that the Angel's responsibilities involve returning the energies and actions of Creation back toward the Divine. This corresponds to the *internalization* of the Angel's qualities in the human being. "S" indicates that the Angel's energies and functions are neither ascending nor descending but stabilized within its own Sephira—and therefore in a state of stability within us.

Angel's sign and Ruling planet

These denote the astrological conditions existing during the moment when the Angel originally emanated from the Divine through the 12 houses of the zodiac. An Angel's name corresponds to its qualities and functions on the human plane, as well as the qualities of its astrological correspondences.

Sephira and Ruling planet

These pertain to the sphere of Divine Energy in which the Angel "resides" on the Tree of Life. The Sephira's primary quality and ruling planet further influence the qualities and functions of all the Angels that reside within the Sephira.

Choir and Archangel

The Archangel is the "head" Angel of each Sephira that governs the respective Choir of Angels residing within it. The Archangel's qualities and functions are carried out in detail by the eight Angels whose energies are less subtle (a heavier vibration) than that of the Archangel, which makes them more accessible to interaction with human beings.

incarnation Days (physical plane)

This is the five-day period during the year when the Angel expresses particular qualities of Physical Manifestation of the Divine and Its Will and Purpose, which also correspond to particular qualities and functions in the human physical realm of birth, will, and life purpose.

Heart Days (emotional plane)

Heart days are the five one-day periods during the year when the Angel expresses particular qualities of Divine Love. They also correspond to particular qualities and functions of love and the use and challenges of human emotions.

intellect Time (mental plane)[2]

This is the 20-minute period in the 24-hour day when the Angel expresses particular qualities of Divine Intellect, which also correspond to particular qualities and functions of intellect on the human plane. Note that we may work with all three of our Birth Angels on any given day during the 20-minute periods of their Intellect dominion. Those born at a cusp time (on the hour or 20 minutes before or after) will have two Intellect Angels.

virtues

Virtues are the "positive," creative, higher-vibration, light-/life-/love-affirming qualities of the Divine that the Angel embodies and which we may partake of by invoking (asking), imbibing (receiving), and ultimately embodying (becoming) that Angel. The Virtues are listed in descending order from the highest spiritual expression and application to the practical and professional applications.

---

[2] There are discrepancies in the dates of governing attributed to the Angels with different sources. I have used the dating system used by the works of Kabaleb and Haziel, which draw from materials on the tradition discovered in the 1975 excavation of the twelfth- to fifteenth-century Gerona grotto, as well as the works of certain other mystics and scholars of the time. This system begins the cycle of Angelic dominion with the Spring Solstice, March 21, also the first day of the sign of Aries, which is considered by certain traditions to be correspondent to the creation of the earth.

inversions

Inversions are the "negative," destructive, lower-vibration, light-/life-/love-negating distortions that result from misuse, abuse, or disuse of Divine Virtues/positive qualities. When Inversions are in play, the tradition says that we should not distract or derail ourselves with guilt or judgment. We should rather regard them as symptoms of disharmony/disturbance and therefore as opportunities for conscious purification, realignment, and "at-onement" with ourselves spiritually, mentally, emotionally, and physically.

Kether

DIVINE QUALILTY
CROWN, DIVINE WILL

First expression/manifestation of the "Undifferentiated/
Unknowable Oneness"

ANGELIC ORDER/CHOIR
SERAPHIM

ARCHANGEL
METATRON

HUMAN QUALITY
Enlightenment, All-Oneness, Wholeness, Self and Selflessness,
Altruism, Humility, Will/Urge to Create, Seed-Planting,
Beginning of a New Cycle

HUMAN BODY
HEAD

RULING PLANET
NEPTUNE (First Swirlings)

COLOR
WHITE

ANGELS
1 VEHUIAH—*Will and New Beginnings*
2 JELIEL—*Love and Wisdom*
3 SITAEL—*Construction of Universe/Worlds*
4 ELEMIAH—*Divine Power*
5 MAHASIAH—*Rectification*
6 LELAHEL—*Light (of Understanding)*
7 ACHAIAH—*Patience*
8 CAHETEL—*Divine Blessings*

1 Vehuiah

(vay-HOO-ee-YAH) *Will and New Beginnings* (G)

Angels's Sign/Planet:	Sephira/Ruling Planet:	Choir/Archangel:
Aries/Uranus	Kether/Neptune	Seraphim/Metatron

Incarnation Days:	Heart Days:	Intellect Time:
3/21–25	3/21, 6/3, 8/17, 10/30, 1/9	12:00–12:20 A.M.

VIRTUES

▲ Illumines and inspires with the Internal Fire to abandon the routine of the past, enter upon a new creative cycle, and forge a new future

▲ Helps to open a road through the maze and confusion of impasse toward new objectives, experiences, and creations

▲ Provides the necessary energy and force to master a difficult or complex situation, problem, depression, or illness

▲ Helps to come out "first" in a course of action or confrontation; helps to be the central force in an exploit, event, or trend and initiate the unprecedented or avant-garde

▲ Fosters an ability to always begin again; helps to experience love as if it were the first time

INVERSIONS

▼ Tendency toward a distorted use of will, imposing will on others

▼ Susceptibility to anger, turbulence, impulsiveness

▼ Tendency toward negative or unproductive decisions or actions that change one's life in a negative way

▼ Susceptibility to create or suffer a violent situation stemming from old conflict

2 Jeliel

(JAY-lee-EL)   *Love and Wisdom* (G)

Angel's Sign/Planet:	Sephira/Ruling Planet:	Choir/Archangel:
Aries/Saturn	Kether/Neptune	Seraphim/Metatron

Incarnation Days:	Heart Days:	Intellect Time:
3/26–30	3/22, 6/4, 8/18 + 19 A.M.,	12:20–12:40 A.M.
	10/31, 1/10	

VIRTUES

▲ Represents Will, which is motivated by the power of Love and Universal Purpose; encourages nobility of purpose and place on the human plane

▲ Helps to fuel the fire, fertility, and power needed to initiate new beginnings

▲ Helps to resolve problems and difficulties of material reality through the Higher Plane, which originates all solutions

▲ Offers a well of unconditional love and eternal wisdom through which one might never go thirsty

▲ Helps to reestablish the calm that brings clarity and fulfillment of highest desires; helps to prevail over injustice and negative forces and become a great light to others

▲ Unites interior aspects of Sun (masculine) and Moon (feminine) and their outer reflections in relationships; helps conjugal fidelity and triumph of harmony over discord or divisiveness

▲ Instills and amplifies sexuality with the Divine creative force within each of us

INVERSIONS

▼ Tendency toward discord, isolation, separation, divorce

▼ Causes or suffers celibacy, barrenness, self-absorption, and unwillingness to bear or foster children

▼ Displays or is a victim of negative tendencies and morals that oppose cosmic order

▼ Tendency to engage in or suffer shallow sentiments and liaisons

3 Sitael

(SIT-ah-EL) *Construction of Universe/Worlds* (G)

Angel's Sign/Planet:	Sephira/Ruling Planet:	Choir/Archangel:
Aries/Jupiter	Kether/Neptune	Seraphim/Metatron

Incarnation Days:	Heart Days:	Intellect Time:
3/31–4/4	3/23, 6/5, 8/19 P.M. + 20, 11/1, 1/11	12:40–1:00 A.M.

VIRTUES

▲ Represents the "Master Builder," which manifests the will and harmony of the Divine Architect; helps to foster the ability to engineer and construct noble works in the world, as well as one's own "inner city"

▲ Helps to overcome all adversity and generously inspire and help others to do the same

▲ Helps to protect against those who would pervert, degrade, deplete, and deconstruct good works

▲ Fosters a love of Truth and a desire to honor one's word/promises

▲ Helps to recognize and build upon newly emerging truths that may add to or confirm prior truths

▲ Helps to become a benefactor with legislative and directorial powers

INVERSIONS

▼ Inclination to pervert, despoil, deconstruct, and cause what has been built to fall to ruins

▼ Displays untrustworthiness and a lack of integrity or authenticity

▼ Tendency toward ignoble encounters and self-serving strategies and objectives

▼ Tendency to provoke or suffer hypocrisy, ingratitude, or adverse judgments in favor of opponent

4 Elemiah

(eh-LEM-ee-YAH)   *Divine Power* (G)

Angel's Sign/Planet:	Sephira/Ruling Planet:	Choir/Archangel:
Aries/Mars	Kether/Neptune	Seraphim/Metatron

Incarnation Days:	Heart Days:	Intellect Time:
4/5–9	3/24, 6/6, 8/21, 11/2, 1/12	1:00–1:20 A.M.

VIRTUES

▲ Helps to balance the Elements within by exposing inner saboteurs and usurpers (earth) in order to overcome torments and tempests of the soul (air) caused by conflicts between emotional and spiritual integrity (water) and desires/urges/impulses (fire)

▲ Helps to grow the Fruit of the Tree of Life within, which contains the seeds of spirituality that permit Divinity to express Itself from within the veiled context of humanity

▲ Helps give the power to realign one's actions to higher values and facilitate coexistence of divine and human nature

▲ Helps to use difficult relationships and encounters with people as opportunities to reconcile and resolve one's own inner conflicts

▲ Helps to enjoy life as an industrious, happily enterprising "voyage"

▲ Helps to harness and utilize internal forces with the precision of a machine and be successful in businesses involving machines

INVERSIONS

▼ Tendency to lead a stormy, chaotic life and to abuse or be abused and weakened by power

▼ Beginning of a period of destruction, encounters with a "bad seed," defeat, bankruptcy, setbacks, or ruin of enterprises

▼ Aptitude for scrap metal occupations

5 Mahasiah

(mah-HA-see-YAH)   *Rectification* (G)

Angel's Sign/Planet:	Sephira/Ruling Planet:	Choir/Archangel:
Aries/Sun	Kether/Neptune	Seraphim/Metatron
Incarnation Days:	Heart Days:	Intellect Time:
4/10–14	3/25, 6/7, 8/22, 11/3, 1/13	1:20–1:40 A.M.

VIRTUES

▲ Gives the capacity to straighten or correct what is about to go crooked before it materializes

▲ Helps to rectify errors with ourselves and others, restore harmony, and live in peace

▲ Helps to learn easily, and to connect the messages behind everyday events with transcendental truths

▲ Helps to analyze dreams and details of daily life as instructions in the profound

▲ Helps to achieve immediate gratification when desires concern spiritual motives and goals

▲ Helps to develop good character and a passion for honest pleasures, which may be reflected in a robust and vital physical appearance

▲ Fosters a tendency toward esoteric sciences, occult philosophy, theology, liberal arts, and initiatic (mystery) schools

INVERSIONS

▼ Tendency to take the wrong road and to consort with the ignorant and immoral

▼ Tendency for sexual life to be intense and exhausting; susceptibility for precarious health of body and soul

▼ Vocation in formal, restrictive aspect of religion/priesthood to escape reality and concerns of the world

6 Lelahel

(LAY-la-HEL)   *Light (of Understanding)* (G)

Angel's Sign/Planet:	Sephira/Ruling Planet:	Choir/Archangel:
Aries/Venus	Kether/Neptune	Seraphim/Metatron

Incarnation Days:	Heart Days:	Intellect Time:
4/15–20	3/26, 6/8, 8/23, 11/4, 1/14	1:40–2:00 A.M.

VIRTUES

▲ Gives access to the source of creation that births and develops knowledge, understanding, consciousness, and lucidity

▲ Helps to internalize the shining light that engenders shining love, which is also reflected externally as beauty, and draws the attraction/admiration of others

▲ Helps to use external difficulties to elevate oneself within

▲ Cultivates inner richness: condensation of light is symbolized by gold (alchemy), which corresponds to the light of understanding that transforms base human mettle into golden thoughts and deeds

▲ Fosters an ability to use the divine healing properties of light to aid in therapy and recovery from maladies

▲ Helps to facilitate love, renown, scientific knowledge, artistic dexterity, and inspiration

INVERSIONS

▼ Harbors ambition for what is not earned or is beyond one's capacity—like wanting to be at the top of a mountain without being willing or able to make the climb

▼ Tendency to seek fortune and success by illicit, forged means

▼ Tendency to be in unstable situations and affairs; potential for immediate spectacular results that ultimately fail or go to ruin with possible danger of imprisonment

▼ Use of personal charm and personality for hidden, impure motives

7 Achaiah

(a-KA-hee-YAH) *Patience* (G)

Angel's Sign/Planet:	Sephira/Ruling Planet:	Choir/Archangel:
Taurus/Mercury	Kether/Neptune	Seraphim/Metatron

Incarnation Days:	Heart Days:	Intellect Time:
4/21–25	3/27, 6/9, 8/24, 11/5, 1/15	2:00–2:20 A.M.

VIRTUES

▲ Brings a state of attentive stillness whereby one can discover secrets of nature and create new paths, horizons, and purposes leading to success and recognition

▲ Helps to use periods of waiting for productive activity and endeavors

▲ Fosters and perpetuates the light of understanding, bringing external manifestation of inner knowledge and discernment between what is useful and what is not

▲ Aids industry of all kinds and helps to start the machinery needed to effect a productive course of action

▲ Gives a propensity for instruction in all that is useful; helps with discovery of new functional processes for art and the artisan, and aids in the execution of difficult tasks

▲ Cultivates the desire to share what is discovered and learned

▲ Influences television, radio, media, publishing

INVERSIONS

▼ Tendency toward restlessness, impatience, ignorance, negligence, laxity, and carelessness

▼ Exhibits passive waiting for things to be handled or given; easily gives up, resigns, or relinquishes

▼ Lack of interest or desire to understand new concepts, situations, or sensibilities so as not to be disturbed in pleasures or habits

8 Cahetel

(KA-heh-TEL)   *Divine Blessings* (G)

Angel's Sign/Planet:	Sephira/Ruling Planet:	Choir/Archangel:
Taurus/Moon	Kether/Neptune	Seraphim/Metatron

Incarnation Days:	Heart Days:	Intellect Time:
4/26–30	3/28, 6/10, 8/25, 11/6, 1/16	2:20–2:40 A.M.

VIRTUES

▲ Brings divine inspiration and blessing to efforts, experiences, and work, especially when the Divine Design is recognized in all that is done

▲ Helps to nourish, transform, and liberate way of living so that inner terrain is fertile and productive

▲ Brings favorable agricultural conditions (sufficient sun, rain, fertile soil) to ensure fruition and abundance of harvest, as well as a balance of other elements needed for basic human and animal subsistence

▲ Fosters enjoyment of "the hunt," which symbolizes the conquering or expelling of base or animalistic tendencies of inner nature

▲ Facilitates enjoyment, acquisition, and success in various terrains of world affairs, agriculture, and country living

INVERSIONS

▼ Exhibits listlessness, moodiness, shallow use of wealth, stagnation

▼ Displays excessive will, aggression, stubbornness, dominance, and arrogance

▼ Fosters interference or opposition to cosmic laws and imbalance of the four elements (earth/air/fire/water), which can be reflected externally as adverse agricultural conditions such as heat waves, torrential rains, flooding, polluted irrigation waters, hailstorms, fire, predatory insects, and other scourges of nature

▼ Fosters base, self-serving tendencies; victim or perpetrator of malice and meanness

Chokmah

DIVINE QUALILTY
WISDOM
(containing all-encompassing Divine Thought that precedes form)

ANGELIC ORDER/CHOIR
CHERUBIM

ARCHANGEL
RAZIEL

HUMAN QUALITIES
Pure undefined thought that precedes created form,
connectedness, and collaboration with the "Other" which
completes the "Two" that must exist in order to create a Third

HUMAN BODY
BRAIN

RULING PLANET
URANUS

COLOR
GRAY

ANGELS
9 HAZIEL—*Divine Mercy and Forgiveness*
10 ALADIAH—*Divine Grace*
11 LAUVIAH—*Victory*
12 HAHAIAH—*Refuge, Shelter*
13 YEZALEL—*Fidelity, Loyalty, and Allegiance*
14 MEBAHEL—*Truth, Liberty, and Justice*
15 HARIEL—*Purification*
16 HAKAMIAH—*Loyalty*

9 Haziel

(HA-zee-EL)   *Divine Mercy and Forgiveness* (S)

Angel's Sign/Planet:	Sephira/Ruling Planet:	Choir/Archangel:
Taurus/Uranus	Chokmah/Uranus	Cherubim/Raziel

Incarnation Days:	Heart Days:	Intellect Time:
5/1– 5	3/29, 6/11, 8/26, 11/7, 1/17	2:40–3:00 A.M.

VIRTUES

▲ Brings primordial beneficent impulse of forgiveness and mercy that precedes and absolves all error and reflects the love of the Divine for Humanity

▲ Helps to be merciful and pardoning to self and others through sincerity of heart

▲ Brings healing and freedom from the weight and misery of past mistakes, karmic debts, and bonds

▲ Helps to remove rancor and resentment; restores innocence and purity

▲ Brings grace to one's efforts and wisdom and knowledge for new beginnings and a new life

▲ Helps to facilitate friendship and patronage from the illustrious

▲ Governs sincerity, good faith, promises, pardons, and reconciliations among individuals and nations

INVERSIONS

▼ Perpetrator or victim of hatred, hypocrisy, and enmity

▼ Perpetuates lack of mercy and forgiveness for self or others

▼ Causes or suffers broken promises and irreconcilable relationships and situations

10 Aladiah

(a-LA-dee-YAH)   *Divine Grace* (R)

Angel's Sign/Planet:	Sephira/Ruling Planet:	Choir/Archangel:
Taurus/Saturn	Chokmah/Uranus	Cherubim/Raziel

Incarnation Days:	Heart Days:	Intellect Time:
5/6–10	3/30, 6/12 + 13 A.M., 8/27, 11/8, 1/18	3:00–3:20 A.M.

VIRTUES

▲ Helps love to "penetrate" and fulfill or temper law, dogma, tradition, rules

▲ Helps to forgive karmic debt and so-called sin, faults, and mistakes of our own, as well as extend empathy and understanding to unconditionally pardon the transgressions or crimes of others

▲ Aids healing of external/physical maladies and the inner discord and disease that engenders them

▲ Facilitates recovery, rehabilitation, and reintegration into society with positive, productive, and successful enterprise

▲ Brings esteem and respect

INVERSIONS

▼ Tendency for negligence, nonchalance, irresponsibility, and unhonored promises

▼ Tendency to display or be a victim of unforgiveness and harsh judgment

▼ Suffers poor health of body, mind, or spirit, as well as fruitless, polluted efforts and enterprises

11 Lauviah

(LO-vee-YAH)   *Victory* (G)

Angel's Sign/Planet:	Sephira/Ruling Planet:	Choir/Archangel:
Taurus/Jupiter	Chokmah/Uranus	Cherubim/Raziel

Incarnation Days:	Heart Days:	Intellect Time:
5/11–15	3/31, 6/13 P.M. + 14, 8/28, 11/9, 1/19	3:20–3:40 A.M.

VIRTUES

▲ Helps to wage an intense, determined fight for triumph over the many battles of existence

▲ Brings a sudden shift in status or circumstances, i.e., the attainment of worldly success by a seemingly insignificant or effortless victory following years of inner dedication and hard work

▲ Helps with favorable acquisition of material goods and successful business affairs during periods of influence in physical/material plane; aids victory in love and elevation of love into altruistic service and spiritual endeavors during days of emotional influence; contributes to triumph of intellectual pursuits during time of mental influence

▲ Endows with a great accumulation of light, knowledge, energy, and clarity, helping to infuse everyday life with higher principles

▲ Brings success for what is deeply and nobly desired; brings renown to the great, talented, and wise who work for the advancement of humankind

INVERSIONS

▼ Tendency for hollow victories or defeat by pride, jealousy, ambition

▼ Tendency for lack of love, material goods, or worldly success

▼ Suffers years of hard and fruitless work or enjoys fame through shallow, self-serving achievements

12 Hahaiah

(ha-HA-ee-YAH)   *Refuge, Shelter* (G)

Angel's Sign/Planet:	Sephira/Ruling Planet:	Choir/Archangel:
Taurus/Mars	Chokmah/Uranus	Cherubim/Raziel

Incarnation Days:	Heart Days:	Intellect Time:
5/16–20	4/1, 6/15, 8/29, 11/10, 1/20	3:40–4:00 A.M.

VIRTUES

▲ Provides an inner haven against destructive tendencies or forces

▲ Helps to protect against adversity and tribulation from the external world and also protect others who are tyrannized or attacked

▲ Helps to reveal and interpret through dreams the mystical workings of the Divine that are "hidden" in daily life; helps to use revelations in dreams to find the "right road" in reality

▲ Helps to turn cosmic knowledge and truth into wisdom, discretion, and kindness

INVERSIONS

▼ Tendency to be victimized by dark, manipulative, destructive forces

▼ Tendency to be untrustworthy and to betray secrets and confidences or be betrayed

▼ Tendency to be misled, to misunderstand the "signs" and wind up in false or precarious situations

13 Yezalel

(YAY-za-LEL) *Fidelity, Loyalty, and Allegiance* (G)

Angel's Sign/Planet:	Sephira/Ruling Planet:	Choir/Archangel:
Gemini/Sun	Chokmah/Uranus	Cherubim/Raziel

Incarnation Days:	Heart Days:	Intellect Time:
5/21–25	4/2, 6/16, 8/30, 11/11, 1/21	4:00–4:20 A.M.

VIRTUES

▲ Helps to practice faithfulness to Divine Love and Wisdom; fosters the desire to choose higher motivations and methods to achieve goals and plans

▲ Brings affinity, loyalty, and fruitfulness in friendship and partnership; helps to draw those of like mind together and bring success to a shared vision

▲ Encourages allegiance to core integrity and sanctity of relationships through conjugal fidelity, reconciliation, and unity

▲ Gives natural affinity for knowledge: helps to learn, understand, and grasp ideas and information easily without intense or prolonged study

▲ Helps to use experience and memory to resolve difficulties by allowing the past to bring perspective and understanding to present challenges

INVERSIONS

▼ Tendency to betray cosmic love, wisdom, and order by ignoble motivations and methods

▼ Tendency to betray and sabotage friendships, partnerships, marriage, and other important relationships, resulting in alienation, separatism, and isolation

▼ Tendency to get bogged down in recriminations of self and others

14 Mebahel

(MAY-ba-HEL)   *Truth, Liberty, and Justice* (G)

Angel's Sign/Planet:	Sephira/Ruling Planet:	Choir/Archangel:
Gemini/Venus	Chokmah/Uranus	Cherubim/Raziel

Incarnation Days:	Heart Days:	Intellect Time:
5/26–31	4/3, 6/17, 8/31, 11/12, 1/22	4:20–4:40 A.M.

VIRTUES

▲ Channels Divine Truth to bring freedom from inner deceivers and justice against internal and external oppressors

▲ Helps to establish or reestablish natural order and ensures alignment and integrity between internal conditions and external results

▲ Brings protection against those who would steal from a "rightful owner," symbolizing the need and ability to eliminate or rehabilitate inner usurpers

▲ Encourages involvement in legal professions, protection of the innocent, and processing of justice, law, and order

INVERSIONS

▼ Tendency to be a victim or a perpetrator of slander, libel, perjury, bearing false witness, and creating or suffering dishonest or delayed legal processes

▼ Suffers inner/outer state of chaos and calamity that results from the distortion of truths

▼ Possibility to be a prisoner of deceit and to have basic well-being and security stolen

15 Hariel

(HA-ree-EL)   *Purification* (G)

Angel's Sign/Planet:	Sephira/Ruling Planet:	Choir/Archangel:
Gemini/Mercury	Chokmah/Uranus	Cherubim/Raziel

Incarnation Days:	Heart Days:	Intellect Time:
6/1–5	4/4, 6/18, 9/1, 11/13, 1/23	4:40–5:00 A.M.

VIRTUES

▲ Reestablishes communication between the eternal sacred Self and the temporal human personality, thereby purifying and elevating attitudes, motives, and actions

▲ Helps to cease ingestion of poor food and toxic substances in order to cleanse oneself physically

▲ Restores a natural and "free" spiritual state and protects against distortions of dogmatic or sectarian ideology

▲ Influences and inspires integrity in religion, art, and science; helps to discover useful inventions and new methods

INVERSIONS

▼ Invites schism, division, animosity, corruption, and controversy

▼ Tendency to impose ideas or ideals upon others, participate in a dangerous sect, or distort and contaminate established religious dogma

▼ Causes or suffers failure, collapse, ruin

16 Hakamiah

(ha-KA-mee-YAH)   *Loyalty* (G)

Angel's Sign/Planet:	Sephira/Ruling Planet:	Choir/Archangel:
Gemini/Moon	Chokmah/Uranus	Cherubim/Raziel

Incarnation Days:	Heart Days:	Intellect Time:
6/6–10	4/5, 6/19, 9/2, 11/14, 1/24[3]	5:00–5:20 A.M.

VIRTUES

▲ Helps to remain faithful to high values and principles; fosters honesty and honorableness in word and deed

▲ Helps to defeat internal traitors, enemies, and oppressors that are mirrored in the external world—especially when aspiring to or defending spiritual ideals

▲ Brings victory, prevents division and sedition, aids as a conciliatory force to integrate opposing factions; also fosters inner victory/mastery/kingship that serves the highest good for self and others

▲ Influences heads of state and leaders of political, military, and social organizations

INVERSIONS

▼ Tendency to distort or compromise values and to betray or be betrayed

▼ An instigator or victim of divisiveness, discord, and revolt

▼ Tendency to lose elections, leadership positions, seniority

---

[3] Simultaneous with 17 LAUVIAH

Binah

DIVINE QUALILTY
UNDERSTANDING
Expression/differentiation of Thought into ideas
and the One into the many

ANGELIC ORDER/CHOIR
THRONES

ARCHANGEL
TZAPHKIEL

HUMAN QUALITIES
Individuation, Creativity, and Expression that begins to give form
and definition to Thought; the last sphere for integration of all
things and beings before they become differentiated into duality
and seemingly diverse creations

HUMAN BODY
MIND

RULING PLANET
SATURN

COLOR
BLACK

ANGELS
17 LAVIAH—*Revelation*
18 CALIEL—*Justice*
19 LEUVIAH—*Expansive Intelligence/Fruition*
20 PAHALIAH—*Redemption*
21 NELCHAEL—*Ardent Desire to Learn*
22 YEIAYEL—*Fame, Renown*
23 MELAHEL—*Healing Capacity*
24 HAHEUIAH—*Protection*

17 Laviah

(LAH-vee-YAH)   *Revelation* (R)

Angel's Sign/Planet:	Sephira/Ruling Planet:	Choir/Archangel:
Gemini/Uranus	Binah/Saturn	Thrones/Tzaphkiel

Incarnation Days:	Heart Days:	Intellect Time:
6/11–15	4/6, 6/20, 9/3, 11/15, 1/24[4]	5:20–5:40 A.M.

VIRTUES

▲ Helps to perceive and instantly understand cosmic truths and great mysteries of life without formal study

▲ Brings messages and revelations via dream images and symbols during sleep, when the physical body is disconnected from ego and is therefore more receptive to the higher self

▲ Helps to put aside base desires and dedicate life to higher studies that are conduits for revelation, such as music, poetry, literature, art, and philosophy

▲ Liberates from sadness and conflicts of the spirit that occur when torn between higher and lower energies

▲ Governs arts, esoteric sciences, and wondrous discoveries

INVERSIONS

▼ Fosters poor perception, misunderstanding, bad judgment, deception

▼ Promotes atheism, impiety, religious antipathy, existential ennui

▼ Brings somberness, sadness, meaningless; lack of confidence, enthusiasm, or principle; lack of faith in self and others

▼ Tendency to be involved in unsavory, impure, illicit affairs or activities

---

[4] Simultaneously with 16 HAKAMIAH

18 Caliel

(KA-lee-EL)   *Justice* (S)

Angel's Sign/Planet:	Sephira/Ruling Planet:	Choir/Archangel:
Gemini/Saturn	Binah/Saturn	Thrones/Tzaphkiel

Incarnation Days:	Heart Days:	Intellect Time:
6/16–21	4/7, 6/21, 9/4, 11/16, 1/25	5:40–6:00 A.M.

VIRTUES

▲ Helps to foster an inner understanding of Divine Justice: cultivates discernment, love of truth, integrity, and a natural justice that weighs all sides but does not over-rely on the judgments or opinions of others

▲ Helps to defeat adversity and injustice, reveal culprits and false witnesses, and bring triumph to the innocent

▲ Helps to prevail against a misuse of conscience, i.e., the inner accusers, judges, and guilt that can paralyze true responsibility and corrective action

▲ Helps to develop honest relationships and associations; helps to ensure emotional justice by correcting or repelling disrespectful, dominating, or abusive behavior

▲ Helps to excel in legal professions as a lawyer, judge, prosecutor, magistrate, etc.

INVERSIONS

▼ Perpetrator or victim of scandalous situations and inner or outer villains that dictate low, greedy, self-serving conduct, which is exploitive, disrespectful, and abusive

▼ Tendency to perpetrate or be victimized by unjust accusation, adversity, and melancholy

▼ Tendency to suffer paralyzing guilt and self-condemnation which continues the cycle of condemnation from others

▼ Tendency to manipulate and distort the law and to advocate in the service of self-interests for criminals and other lawbreakers

19 Leuviah

(LOO-vee-YAH)   *Expansive Intelligence/Fruition* (G)

Angel's Sign/Planet:	Sephira/Ruling Planet:	Choir/Archangel:
Cancer/Jupiter	Binah/Saturn	Thrones/Tzaphkiel

Incarnation Days:	Heart Days:	Intellect Time:
6/22–26	4/8, 6/22, 9/5, 11/17, 1/26	6:00–6:20 A.M.

VIRTUES

▲ Helps to cultivate memory and intelligence; expands range of intelligence by using memory of past events and experience to inform and positively influence present thought and action

▲ Helps to reap the fruits of knowledge which carry the seeds of universal intelligence; governs cosmic memory and the history of souls known as "The Akashic Records," "The Book of Life," or "The Book of God's Remembrance"

▲ Brings ability to temper feelings with reason, materialize ideas into practical reality, and manifest great works

▲ Helps to develop traits of cheerfulness, modesty, humility, kindness, willingness to help others, and patience in the face of adversity

▲ Cultivates simplicity of speech, action, and being which enables open, friendly communication with all types of people

▲ Fosters the ability to remember what was forgotten and to succeed in endeavors and professions where memory is important

INVERSIONS

▼ Tendency toward unclear thinking, confused and erratic actions, forgetfulness, hostility

▼ Tendency toward loss, humiliation, sadness, self-pity, debauchery, and despair; suffers a laborious, amoral, and destitute life

▼ Tendency toward love of short duration, seduction followed by abandonment, desire without love, untrustworthiness

20 Pahaliah

(pa-HA-lee-YAH)   *Redemption* (G)

Angel's Sign/Planet:	Sephira/Ruling Planet:	Choir/Archangel:
Cancer/Mars	Binah/Saturn	Thrones/Tzaphkiel

Incarnation Days:	Heart Days:	Intellect Time:
6/27–7/1	4/9, 6/23, 9/6, 11/18, 1/27	6:20–6:40 A.M.

VIRTUES

▲ Works on the emotional plane to develop consciousness of cosmic laws and discernment of high and low (right and wrong) desires and actions

▲ Gives sensibility to choose a higher road, correct and atone for transgressions, surmount difficulties, and transform unproductive and unhealthy desires or tendencies into higher ideals, motives, and behavior

▲ Helps to defeat emotional, spiritual, and physical maladies or difficulties and restore health and productivity

▲ Influences religion, theology, morality, chastity, and piety; encourages religious vocations which provide a professional scenario to practice externally the spiritual integrity which must ultimately be achieved internally

INVERSIONS

▼ Inability or unwillingness to transform and redeem oneself, resulting in a need to dogmatically proselytize and convert others

▼ Tendency to take the "low road," engage in repeated transitory and shallow liaisons, and to be a prisoner of base desires or compulsions

▼ Governs the unprincipled, atheists, libertines, renegades, and reprobates

21 Nelchael

(NEL-ka-EL)   *Ardent Desire to Learn* (G)

Angel's Sign/Planet:	Sephira/Ruling Planet:	Choir/Archangel:
Cancer/Sun	Binah/Saturn	Thrones/Tzaphkiel

Incarnation Days:	Heart Days:	Intellect Time:
7/2–6	4/10, 6/24, 9/7, 11/19, 1/28	6:40–7:00 A.M.

VIRTUES

▲ Gives a natural and passionate desire to acquire knowledge and to learn the mechanics, meaning, and origin of things

▲ Helps to develop the ability to discern the truth of things and to elevate the use of knowledge in earthly situations and scenarios

▲ Helps to use the powers of truth, knowledge, and wisdom to repel discordant and destructive ignorance and other life-negating energies

▲ Helps to develop powers of focus and concentration and the ability to excel on exams and other testing situations

▲ Gives an aptitude for astronomy, geometry, geography, and abstract sciences, as well as philosophy and literature, particularly poetry

INVERSIONS

▼ Tendency to suffer from or behave with ignorance, error, and prejudice

▼ Tendency to be stubborn, to sacrifice aptitude for attitude, and cling to the right to be wrong

▼ Tendency to disregard one's own intelligence and be influenced and manipulated by the judgment of others

▼ Propensity for paralysis and stagnation of efforts or results

22 Yeiayel

(YAY-ah-YEL)   *Fame, Renown* (G)

Angel's Sign/Planet:	Sephira/Ruling Planet:	Choir/Archangel:
Cancer/Venus	Binah/Saturn	Thrones/Tzaphkiel
Incarnation Days:	**Heart Days:**	**Intellect Time:**
7/7–11	4/11, 6/25, 9/8, 11/20, 1/29	7:00–7:20 A.M.

VIRTUES

▲ Cultivates fame and fortune, particularly in areas that benefit society such as the arts, science, and politics

▲ Brings industriousness, inventiveness, determination, diplomacy, and business skills that lead to success

▲ Helps to inspire and encourage the endeavors and aims of others

▲ Encourages liberalism, philanthropy, and exchange of information and energy to develop new enterprises and partnerships

▲ Influences maritime expeditions and discoveries and protects against tempests and navigational disaster; also brings the equilibrium needed in the sea of emotions to navigate through stalls and storms and successfully "bring the ship to shore"

INVERSIONS

▼ Denial of success and recognition, victim or perpetrator of piracy, profiteering of monetary or material assets

▼ Tendency toward usurping the acclaim due to others

▼ Plagued by agitated and contradictory feelings and sentiments

▼ Commits outrage and injustice, promotes tyrannical social doctrine

23 Melahel

(MAY-la-HEL)   *Healing Capacity* (G)

Angel's Sign/Planet:	Sephira/Ruling Planet:	Choir/Archangel:
Cancer/Mercury	Binah/Saturn	Thrones/Tzaphkiel

Incarnation Days:	Heart Days:	Intellect Time:
7/12–16	4/12, 6/26, 9/9, 11/21, 1/30	7:20–7:40 A.M.

VIRTUES

▲ Helps to understand healing properties and application of medicinal plants and other natural remedies; fosters an ability to teach the science of herbal medicine to others

▲ Creates a connectedness to water and things that grow out of the earth

▲ Helps to master emotions (water) with thoughts (air)

▲ Helps to be in rightful place without envy or desire to be somewhere else

▲ Encourages love of peace and opposes the use of weapons, force, or violence; helps to conquer or survive dangerous situations

▲ Fosters the tendency to be honorable and noble in actions

▲ Fosters an ability to heal in professional or private context

INVERSIONS

▼ Tendency for polluted enterprises and efforts, contaminated results, and outgrowths

▼ Tendency for corrupted feelings, contagious/dangerous maladies, and ineffective healing

▼ Tendency for dissension and disruption

24 Haheuiah

(ha-HOO-ee-YAH)   *Protection* (G)

Angel's Sign/Planet:	Sephira/Ruling Planet:	Choir/Archangel:
Cancer/Moon	Binah/Saturn	Thrones/Tzaphkiel

Incarnation Days:	Heart Days:	Intellect Time:
7/17–22	4/13, 6/27, 9/10, 11/22, 1/31	7:40–8:00 A.M.

VIRTUES

▲ Provides protection and due process of law for those accused of crimes committed unintentionally so that justice can be determined; delays the discovery of secret transgressions to allow opportunity for atonement and transformation

▲ Triggers conscience and conscious responsibility/awareness between perpetrator and victim; helps to draw the grace and compassion of the Divine for understanding and healing; intervenes with exiles, fugitives, and the condemned

▲ Protects against internal beasts or "Forces of the Abyss," which may also be mirrored in external/worldly foes

▲ Fosters love of Truth and study or work with exact sciences (mathematics, chemistry, physics, astronomy); develops sincerity of words and actions which attempt to discover or represent truths

INVERSIONS

▼ Tendency to engage with dangerous entities, criminals, and violent or illicit activities

▼ Tendency to be a perpetrator or a victim of crime/violence

▼ Susceptibility to inner "demons" or external tyranny

Chesed

DIVINE QUALILTY
LOVE and MERCY
Unlimited Expansion, Kindness, and Compassion

ANGELIC ORDER/CHOIR
DOMINATIONS

ARCHANGEL
TZADKIEL

HUMAN QUALITIES
Lovingkindness, Healing, Nurturing, Receptivity,
Expansion, Forgiveness, Generosity

HUMAN BODY
RIGHT ARM

RULING PLANET
JUPITER

COLOR
BLUE

ANGELS
25 NITH-HAIAH—*Spiritual Wisdom and Magic*
26 HAAIAH—*Political Science and Ambition*
27 YERATEL—*Propagation of the Light*
28 SEHEIAH—*Longevity*
29 REIYEL—*Liberation*
30 OMAEL—*Fertility, Multiplicity*
31 LECABEL—*Intellectual Talent*
32 VASARIAH—*Clemency and Equilibrium*

25 Nith-haiah

(NIT-ha-YAH) *Spiritual Wisdom and Magic* (R)

Angel's Sign/Planet:	Sephira/Ruling Planet:	Choir/Archangel:
Leo/Uranus	Chesed/Jupiter	Dominations/ Tzadkiel

Incarnation Days:	Heart Days:	Intellect Time:
7/23–27	4/14, 6/28, 9/11, 11/23, 2/1	8:00–8:20 A.M.

VIRTUES

▲ Elevates sight to penetrate Higher Wisdom and contemplate cosmic currents, seasons, and cycles

▲ Instills desire to seek truth and the wisdom of cosmic order, as reflected in the cyclical and abundant "magic" of the Divine to (1) seed, (2) germinate, (3) blossom, and (4) bear fruit

▲ Brings revelations through dreams and conducts knowledge through emotions activated during dreaming

▲ Helps to discover and master esoteric truths and mysteries and become a conductor of wisdom to others

▲ Helps to hear glorious melodies and music of the spheres and to experience the immense grandeur of Creation

▲ Influences toward places and conditions of peace and solitude

INVERSIONS

▼ Tendency to disturb and reverse the seasons and cycles of creation and bring destruction and chaos to cosmic order

▼ Tendency to be possessed by black magic, sorcery, alignment with dark forces, and renunciation of God in order to do harm to creatures and creations

▼ Prone to nightmares, despair, malcontent, mal-doing, and ruin

26 Haaiah

(HA-ee-YAH)   *Political Science and Ambition* (R)

Angel's Sign/Planet:	Sephira/Ruling Planet:	Choir/Archangel:
Leo/Saturn	Chesed/Jupiter	Dominations/ Tzadkiel

Incarnation Days:	Heart Days:	Intellect Time:
7/28–8/1	4/15, 6/29, 9/12, 11/24, 2/2	8:20–8:40 A.M.

VIRTUES

▲ Aids in contemplation of the Divine beyond logic and reason; helps to organize the microuniverse of man and societal structures as reflections of the macrocosmic order of Divine Truth and Power

▲ Helps to effect rightful due process and favorable judgments and to protect those who seek truth and justice

▲ Regulates and harmonizes excess tendencies/impulses of desire and thought; helps to establish and maintain the internal order that promotes good health among bodily systems and functions

▲ Helps to develop trustworthiness as an agent/representative/messenger for presentation, decision making, secret expeditions, and the signing of treaties which require maximum discretion

▲ Helps to become a great guide, politician, leader, ambassador, or diplomat with high principles and extraordinary wisdom

INVERSIONS

▼ Portrays self-serving ambition and misuse of political power and dominion, which reflects inability to align with right motivation

▼ Promotes internal/external disorder, conspiracy, anarchy, despotism, traitorous actions, and uncontrollable impulses and tendencies

▼ Brings havoc, disagreement, and disruption among negotiating parties

▼ Suffers illness that results from disturbed and out-of-balance body systems and functions

27 Yeratel

(YEH-ra-TEL)   *Propagation of the Light* (S)

Angel's Sign/Planet:	Sephira/Ruling Planet:	Choir/Archangel:
Leo/Jupiter	Chesed/Jupiter	Dominations/ Tzadkiel

Incarnation Days:	Heart Days:	Intellect Time:
8/2–6	4/16 + 17 A.M., 6/30, 9/13, 11/25, 2/3	8:40–9:00 A.M.

VIRTUES

▲ Brings the Primordial light that spawns and sustains individuals, civilizations, liberty, and justice; helps to disseminate on Earth the light that informs and warms human relations through higher understandings

▲ Brings the light of knowledge that elevates human emotions and thoughts to defeat inner and outer saboteurs

▲ Protects against unjust provocation, accusation, and attack, as well as dispersing negative energies attracted by impure thoughts and deeds

▲ Instills love of peace, justice, science, and the arts; brings distinction through the written or spoken word, as well as in political and social sciences

INVERSIONS

▼ Brings the darkness of ignorance, chaos, and the undermining of civilizations

▼ Tendency toward substance dependencies and slavery to attitudes, habits, ideologies, or persons, as well as intolerance toward others who might threaten these negative attachments

▼ Victim or perpetrator of unjust accusation and attack

▼ Pollutes the realms of science and arts for dark gains

28 Seheiah

(say-HAY-ee-YAH)   *Longevity* (G)

Angel's Sign/Planet:	Sephira/Ruling Planet:	Choir/Archangel:
Leo/Mars	Chesed/Jupiter	Dominations/ Tzadkiel

Incarnation Days:	Heart Days:	Intellect Time:
8/7–12	4/17 P.M. + 18, 7/1, 9/14, 11/26, 2/4	9:00–9:20 A.M.

VIRTUES

▲ Represents "Great healer of the zodiac:" releases body and mind from negative emotions, lethargy, and paralysis so that the life energy of Fire/Light may circulate freely throughout internal organs and tissues to restore them to health and vitality

▲ Brings cooling, healing "water" to prevent or extinguish excess of inner fire caused by suppressing or not expressing the force of will rightly

▲ Fosters a natural capacity to rehabilitate and heal oneself and others; helps to receive miraculous healing

▲ Helps to develop good judgment and discernment through balance of ideas/inspiration (Fire) and emotions/perspective (Water)

▲ Protects against lightning, fire, falls, accidents, and sickness

▲ Brings longevity of life, undertakings, and projects

INVERSIONS

▼ Tendency for suppressed or distorted expression of will, feeling of asphyxiation, and need to escape or distract oneself through the addictive use of drugs, alcohol, and sex

▼ Catastrophic incendiary conditions that turn life into a desert without friends, affection, success, or hope

▼ Danger of fire/burning, serious malady, paralysis

▼ Governed by negativity, poor judgment, and action without reflection or discernment

29 Reiyel

(RAY-ee-YEL)   *Liberation* (G)

Angel's Sign/Planet:	Sephira/Ruling Planet:	Choir/Archangel:
Leo/Sun	Chesed/Jupiter	Dominations/ Tzadkiel

Incarnation Days:	Heart Days:	Intellect Time:
8/13–17	4/19, 7/2, 9/15, 11/27, 2/5	9:20–9:40 A.M.

VIRTUES

▲ Helps to disengage from mundane and material pleasures to elevate the emotional nature and reconnect the Self to Love, Wisdom, Eternal Law, and vital energetic nourishment

▲ Helps to remove obstacles and impediments in order to reach higher summits; helps to find Truth in all things and places, especially work and society

▲ Helps to overcome fears, constricted beliefs, and "bewitchments" to enable opening and movement toward the light

▲ Influences spiritual feelings, philosophy, meditation, and cultivation of Divine Truths

▲ Helps to relax claim on "known worlds" of dogma, tradition, and sovereignty to become a "free citizen" in a universe without boundaries, intolerance, or separatism

INVERSIONS

▼ Unable to discern or live in truth; prisoner of fears, falsities, and bewitchment

▼ Brings fanaticism, hypocrisy, impiety, and irreligious attitudes and actions through propaganda and the promotion of false doctrines

▼ Imitates authenticity, as in "the sound of truth from the lips of a liar" or "a wolf in sheep's clothing"

30 Omael

(O-ma-EL)   *Fertility, Multiplicity* (G)

Angel's Sign/Planet:	Sephira/Ruling Planet:	Choir/Archangel:
Leo/Venus	Chesed/Jupiter	Dominations/ Tzadkiel

Incarnation Days:	Heart Days:	Intellect Time:
8/18–22	4/20, 7/3, 9/16, 11/28, 2/6	9:40–10:00 A.M.

VIRTUES

▲ Helps to sow, reap, and multiply harvest in all things internal (ideas, feelings, consciousness) and external (material, worldly)

▲ Brings fertility to all seed plantings and creations in the human, animal, and plant kingdoms in order to multiply species and perpetuate races and generations; helps with infertility or difficulty conceiving

▲ Brings support and abundance to new enterprises and undertakings; helps to defeat frustration, despair, and depression with patience, fortification, drive, joy, and hope

▲ Influences/helps/brings distinction to chemists, doctors (especially gynecology), surgeons, pharmacologists, and other vocations that help to maintain and prolong a well-functioning healthy life

INVERSIONS

▼ Enemy of propagation of beings, tendency toward extermination, genocide, and cultivation of monstrous phenomena and forms

▼ Destroys, divides, diminishes life and living beings, things, ideas, or enterprises

▼ Promotes the slaughter of animals and reduction of agricultural production

▼ Propensity for short-lived enterprises, sterility, precarious health, despair, and short life

31 Lecabel

(LAY-ka-BEL)   *Intellectual Talent* (G)

Angel's Sign/Planet:	Sephira/Ruling Planet:	Choir/Archangel:
Virgo/Mercury	Chesed/Jupiter	Dominations/ Tzadkiel

Incarnation Days:	Heart Days:	Intellect Time:
8/23–28	4/21, 7/4 + 5 A.M., 9/17, 11/29, 2/7	10:00–10:20 A.M.

VIRTUES

▲ "Muse" for the problem solver: provides insight and intellectual power to develop brilliant strategies and solutions to problems and challenges; helps to salvage and revive enterprises in crisis with lucrative results

▲ Gives power of reason to curb emotional excess and the clarity to illuminate a situation and take appropriate action

▲ Encourages great success and directorship in professions that require mental acuity and strategic planning, i.e., economic, social, military settings; also gives propensity, toward exact sciences such as astronomy, mathematics, and geometry

▲ Helps to extract from oneself and others intellectual, emotional and physical tumors, illnesses, distortions, and disturbances

▲ Endows with talent and energy for initiating, cultivating, and harvesting; also influences work with vegetation and agricultural engineering

INVERSIONS

▼ Misuse of mental powers leading to avarice, usury, and involvement in illicit business and other affairs that promise quick profit/gain (drug trafficking, black marketeering, etc.)

▼ Tendency toward misconstruing/misreading facts or events and entering into precarious or exploitive situations and relationships

▼ Develops strategies and conditions that corrupt, spoil, destroy, and impoverish

32 Vasariah

(va-SAH-ree-YAH)   *Clemency and Equilibrium* (G)

Angel's Sign/Planet:	Sephira/Ruling Planet:	Choir/Archangel:
Virgo/Moon	Chesed/Jupiter	Dominations/
		Tzadkiel

Incarnation Days:	Heart Days:	Intellect Time:
8/29–9/2	4/22, 7/5 P.M. + 6, 9/18,	10:20–10:40 A.M.
	11/30, 2/8	

VIRTUES

▲ Brings the mercy that tempers justice, without which true justice would not be possible

▲ Brings the grace of a mercy that can reform the offender more profoundly than punishment, thereby enabling complete absolution and the restoration of harmony

▲ Protects/intervenes against those who would judge or attack us, as well as encouraging us to not judge ourselves or others too harshly

▲ Fosters ease of speech, amicability, modesty and support of others' success; helps to develop a noble heart and soul that is willing to forgive, forget the bad, and acknowledge the good

▲ Influences professions in law/justice, i.e., lawyers, judges, magistrates, mediators, arbitrators, etc.

INVERSIONS

▼ Tendency toward severity, injustice, ignobility, arrogance, and materialism

▼ Tendency toward distortion of the law, corrupt intentions, and fatal/destructive influence

▼ Harbors increasing negativity that can destroy efforts or enterprise

▼ Tendency to be sick and endure suffering from increasing physical or psychological maladies

Geburah

DIVINE QUALILTY
JUSTICE/JUDGMENT/STRENGTH
Limitation, Contraction

ANGELIC ORDER/CHOIR
POWERS

ARCHANGEL
KAMAEL

HUMAN QUALITIES
Discipline, Structure, Self-Determination, Focus,
Boundaries, Contraction, Judgment, Frugality

HUMAN BODY
LEFT ARM

RULING PLANET
MARS

COLOR
RED

ANGELS
33 YEHUIAH—*Subordination to Higher Order*
34 LEHAHIAH—*Obedience*
35 CHAVAKIAH—*Reconciliation*
36 MENADEL—*Inner/Outer Work*
37 ANIEL—*Breaking the Circle*
38 HAAMIAH—*Ritual and Ceremony*
39 REHAEL—*Filial Submission*
40 YEIAZEL—*Divine Consolation and Comfort*

33 Yehuiah

(yay-HOO-ee-YAH)   *Subordination to Higher Order* (R)

Angel's Sign/Planet:	Sephira/Ruling Planet:	Choir/Archangel:
Virgo/Uranus	Geburah/Mars	Powers/Kamael

Incarnation Days:	Heart Days:	Intellect Time:
9/3–7	4/23, 7/7, 9/19, 12/1, 2/9	10:40–11:00 A.M.

VIRTUES

▲ Helps to discern value, position, order of things, and rightful place in that order; helps to prioritize and to respect the process that arrives at a new place in due time

▲ Implants the Christic dynamic in the Higher Self: helps to establish an inner hierarchy that will serve the soul's purposes on this earthly plane, as in: "the first shall be last, and the last shall be first," "the meek shall inherit the earth," "the servant shall be the master," or "the riches of the heart are greater than those of the pocket"

▲ Helps to regulate impulses, drives, and intensity expressed by physical and emotional aspects in order that the soul's agenda may be expressed

▲ Exposes inner betrayers and restores authority to the Higher Self and what is true and essential; until self-betrayal is cured, the battle may take place in the external world as people or situations involving betrayal

▲ Encourages a desire to be of service and gives support to altruistic endeavors

▲ Helps to honor obligations, contracts, and alliances; protects against those who would deceive or cheat

INVERSIONS

▼ Brings insubordination, sedition, rebellion, disrespect, and disregard of authorities and civil or moral law

▼ Brings erosion of higher values for satisfaction of egoistic desires, ambitions, and power to the detriment of self and others

▼ Causes or suffers conflict with one's superiors, organizations, or hierarchy within family

▼ Subversiveness that can bring criminal activities and imprisonment

34 Lehahiah

(lay-HA-hee-YAH)   *Obedience* (R)

Angel's Sign/Planet:	Sephira/Ruling Planet:	Choir/Archangel:
Virgo/Saturn	Geburah/Mars	Powers/Kamael
Incarnation Days:	**Heart Days:**	**Intellect Time:**
9/8–12	4/24, 7/8, 9/20 + 21 A.M., 12/2, 2/10	11:00–11:20 A.M.

VIRTUES

▲ Helps to correct internal and external injustice and nurture faith in cosmic law to ultimately right all injustice

▲ Helps to shift internal power—from spirit to heart to mind to body—whenever the soul's growth requires any one aspect to be leading for a time

▲ Helps to obey superiors and established order, despite apparent unjustness, in order to allow time for a complete picture or "whole story" to be revealed

▲ Helps to dissolve anger and the urge for retribution when obstacles prevent the fulfillment of desires; brings acceptance and realization that what appears in our lives externally is a mirror of what was first engendered internally

▲ Influences heads of state, nobility, etc., to maintain harmony, understanding, peace, and obedience of "subjects" in order to prevent or cure discord, chaos, and violence from unruly impulses or forces

▲ Helps to succeed in professions requiring obedience, integrity, and trustworthiness, as in associations with kings, princes, presidents, ministers, and directors of government or business

INVERSIONS

▼ Promotes misunderstanding, discord, disagreement, conflict, and war with established power(s) and between heads of state and political order or business

▼ Can betray, deceive, and provoke the ruin of a nation if administrative pollution reaches high enough

▼ Causes a climate of hostility in opposition to projects, plans, strategies, orders

35 Chavakiah

(cha-VA-kee-YAH)   *Reconciliation* (R)

Angel's Sign/Planet:	Sephira/Ruling Planet:	Choir/Archangel:
Virgo/Jupiter	Geburah/Mars	Powers/Kamael

Incarnation Days:	Heart Days:	Intellect Time:
9/13–17	4/25, 7/9, 9/21 P.M. + 22, 12/3, 2/11	11:20 - 11:40 A.M.

VIRTUES

▲ Helps to heal karma: transforms and lightens the effect of past events into positive awareness and results; helps to resolve unfinished situations and emotions so energies may be free to assist present and future activities

▲ Helps to heal the internal self-offense that lies behind external conflict; helps to reconcile and heal personality aspects that constitute the "inner family" of past and present selves

▲ Helps in matters of last wills, successions, and divisiveness to bring peace and harmony among family members in order to pass on beneficial heritage, legacies, patronage, and settlements

▲ Helps to recover and realize projects that were unfinished, abandoned, or previously impossible

▲ Influences mediators and arbitrators; helps society to reconcile disputes, races, and cultures, and to mingle ideas from the past into the present and future

INVERSIONS

▲ Tendency to become a prisoner of the past resulting from unresolved conflicts with people/situations; suffers negative conditions, attitudes, judgments, and poor health in present life resulting from negative past experiences

▲ Discord among family members, warring within self among opposing desires and agendas

▲ Promotes or perpetuates societal and political discord and warring

▲ Becomes either an instigator or a victim of morally and materially unjust and ruinous processes

36 Menadel

(MEH-na-DEL)   *Inner/Outer Work* (S)

Angel's Sign/Planet:	Sephira/Ruling Planet:	Choir/Archangel:
Virgo/Mars	Geburah/Mars	Powers/Kamael

Incarnation Days:	Heart Days:	Intellect Time:
9/18–23	4/26, 7/10, 9/23, 12/4, 2/12	11:40–12:00 noon

VIRTUES

▲ Helps to develop a true calling that reflects the soul's higher purposes and potentials as well as an individual's innate talents and skills

▲ Helps to do the inner work that clears obstacles and cleans motivations, so that one's outer work can be expressed fully without being contaminated by unresolved/unhealed fears, issues, attitudes, or concerns

▲ Helps to ground contemplative tendencies so that thoughts and ideas can be materialized into fruitful actions

▲ Helps to foster integrity, harmony, and willingness between the inner and outer "workplace" so that inner growth may ultimately result in higher career levels

▲ Helps to develop a responsible work ethic and maintain employment and way of life; helps to put an end to a period of dormancy, exile, or loss of work

INVERSIONS

▼ Tendency to be trapped in work that is unsuited to one's talents, skills, or interests, which creates low performance levels, taking credit for someone else's work, or other fraudulent representations

▼ Disruption and disharmony in the workplace due to individual dissatisfaction and conflicts between employees

▼ Inner chaos, confusion, or disinterest in any kind of interior emotional or spiritual work; inability to focus ideas into fruitful action

37 Aniel

(AH-nee-EL)   *Breaking the Circle* (G)

Angel's Sign/Planet:	Sephira/Ruling Planet:	Choir/Archangel:
Libra/Sun	Geburah/Mars	Powers/Kamael

Incarnation Days:	Heart Days:	Intellect Time:
9/24–28	4/27, 7/11, 9/24, 12/5, 2/13	12:00–12:20 P.M.

VIRTUES

▲ Helps to draw the spiritual presence that can open new emotional avenues of thought and response, which will then open new doors of opportunity and action

▲ Helps to bring freedom from living as a karmic "hostage" to repetitive and nonproductive cycles of feelings, thoughts, and actions, as well as debilitating dependencies and outdated, stifling influences

▲ Helps to access secrets of the natural world and its cycles, particularly nature's capacity for rebirth

▲ Influences new discoveries and progressive concepts in the arts and sciences

▲ Helps to achieve success and renown based on wisdom, talent, and achievement

INVERSIONS

▼ Propensity for clinging to status quo and old patterns despite negative effects or updated trends in creativity, business practices, and production

▼ Tendency toward fearfulness and stubbornness; causes or suffers perversity and charlatanism in resistance to new concepts or applications

▼ Tendency toward materialism and stifling traditionalism

38 Haamiah

(ha-AH-mee-YAH)   *Ritual and Ceremony* (G)

Angel's Sign/Planet:	Sephira/Ruling Planet:	Choir/Archangel:
Libra/Venus	Geburah/Mars	Powers/Kamael

Incarnation Days:	Heart Days:	Intellect Time:
9/29–10/3	4/28, 7/12, 9/25, 12/6, 2/14	12:20–12:40 P.M.

VIRTUES

▲ Helps to experience life as a meaningful rite of passage; encourages the use of daily ritual to instruct, inspire, and uplift everyday existence toward higher awareness

▲ Inscribes ritual and sacred gestures internally in accord with Eternal Self to establish a personal initiatic path and "science for living"

▲ Helps to obtain and transform treasures of heaven (above, inner) into earthly (below, external) fruits:

Divine/above Treasures	becomes:	Human/below Fruit
Will/Purpose		*Initiative/Experience*
Wisdom/Understanding		*Love/Unity with all creatures*
Intelligence ˙		*Comprehension of cosmic laws*
Expression		*Manifestation*

▲ Helps to neutralize excessive accumulation of dangerous, destructive powers; gives a sudden jolt of "light" to mental and emotional planes that can transform an individual to a higher level (for example, that which changed Saul to Paul on the road to Damascus)

▲ Helps to find the perfect complement, partner, love

▲ Influences all rituals and ceremonies of religious and esoteric schools and helps practitioners and conductors of ritual events

INVERSIONS

▼ Blockage and stagnation of vital sacred energy within individuals and groups that can cause an imbalanced, distorted shell that focuses on conformity to dogma and law rather than the power of love and grace to transform

▼ Hollow practice of ritual that is meaningless and oppressive; distorted use of ritual for black arts and dark purposes

▼ Tendency to spoil and pollute love and other partner-relationships

▼ Danger of being struck by lightning or suffering electrocution

39 Rehael

(RAY-ha-EL)   Filial Submission (G)

Angel's Sign/Planet:	Sephira/Ruling Planet:	Choir/Archangel:
Libra/Mercury	Geburah/Mars	Powers/Kamael
Incarnation Days:	**Heart Days:**	**Intellect Time:**
10/4–8	4/29, 7/13, 9/26, 12/7, 2/15	12:40–1:00 P.M.

VIRTUES

▲ Helps to continue succession of purpose and essential energy as symbolized by the Tree of Life, in which each branch (Sephira/sphere of energy) carries on the essence that came before it and also expresses renewed vitality through new variations and combinations

▲ Governs the generations and hierarchies of filial obedience, love, and respect wherein every son and daughter is charged with carrying on the heritage of family essence, design, and integrity

▲ Helps to foster good health and long life by keeping a love-and-life-affirming parent-child relationship

▲ Helps to heal mental maladies caused by rebellion or distortion of natural internal hierarchy, and keeps the physical channels of circulation (for liquids, solids, and gases) clear and healthy

▲ Helps to maintain productive hierarchies in business, politics, and society to ensure fruitful ongoingness

INVERSIONS

▼ Causes or suffers continually suppressed or expressed turmoil that can result in separation and alienation from parents as well as self-alienation, depression, and anxiety

▼ Rebellion, disobedience, and disregard of parents from one generation to the next, which slowly weakens and destroys family structure and mars the ability of children to become responsive and loving parents

▼ Disobedience of subordinate internal aspects against dominant order, causing mental and emotional anguish and physical disease

▼ Causes or suffers cruelty, child abuse, and cessation of generations wherein love becomes hate and life becomes death via infanticide, patricide, suicide

40 Yeiazel

(YAY-ah-ZEL)   *Divine Consolation and Comfort* (G)

Angel's Sign/Planet:	Sephira/Ruling Planet:	Choir/Archangel:
Libra/Moon	Geburah/Mars	Powers/Kamael

Incarnation Days:	Heart Days:	Intellect Time:
10/9–13	4/30, 7/14, 9/27, 12/8, 2/16	1:00–1:20 P.M.

VIRTUES

▲ Brings relief and comfort when negative forces have been vanquished and hard work bears long-awaited fruits

▲ Helps to begin a new period of creation

▲ Helps to calm the emotional deluge that can occur when feelings, passions, and desires drown out higher impulses and cause imbalances

▲ Helps to develop an ability to transmit to others via written or spoken word the treasures of experience and lessons learned during a voyage of self-discovery

▲ Facilitates communication, publishing companies, libraries, and authors; particularly effective for writing, submission of manuscripts and publication, as well as reading and learning from authors' works that explain interior processes via personal memoir

INVERSIONS

▼ Generates all negative qualities or conditions of body and soul, including a deluge of emotions into areas not in their domain, thereby creating imbalance, poor health, even death

▼ Tendency for pessimism, negative thoughts, ruinous events, or long and draining enterprises with lack of energy to regroup, reorganize, or repair

▼ Distorts, corrupts, or inhibits communication from divine or earthly "messengers" that might otherwise alleviate fear or suffering

SEPHIRA 6

Tiphareth

DIVINE QUALILTY

BEAUTY/COMPASSION/HARMONY

Balances Mercy and Judgment

ANGELIC ORDER/CHOIR

VIRTUES

ARCHANGEL

RAPHAEL

HUMAN QUALITIES

Balancing, Life-affirming, Wise Compassion, Light, Warmth,
Mutuality, Reciprocity, the Natural Beauty of Harmony

HUMAN BODY

HEART/TORSO

RULING PLANET

SUN

COLOR

YELLOW/GOLD

ANGELS

41 HAHAHEL—*Mission*

42 MIKAEL—*Political Authority and Order*

43 VEULIAH—*Prosperity*

44 YELAHIAH—*Karmic Warrior*

45 SEHALIAH—*Motivation and Willfulness*

46 ARIEL—*Perceiver and Revealer*

47 ASALIAH—*Contemplation*

48 MIHAEL—*Fertility, Fruitfulness*

41 Hahahel

(HA-ha-HEL)   *Mission* (R)

Angel's Sign/Planet:	Sephira/Ruling Planet:	Choir/Archangel:
Libra/Uranus	Tiphareth/Sun	Virtues/Raphael

Incarnation Days:	Heart Days:	Intellect Time:
10/14–18	5/1, 7/15, 9/28, 12/9, 2/17	1:20–1:40 P.M.

VIRTUES

▲ Protector of true Christianity and all practitioners representing Christic principles of love and forgiveness as a direct birthright for ALL people; helps to eradicate boundaries and separation of peoples or groups due to race, religion, and other differences

▲ Helps to engage the Christic spirit and express universal love, forgiveness, wisdom, generosity, power, and glory for the enrichment of others

▲ Helps to transform the sacrilegious of the external world; helps to thwart or cure actions that reflect disregard of the Higher Self and its purposes

▲ Helps to create or venture into a "new world," enterprise, or endeavor that is divinely inspired and beneficial to society

▲ Helps to see the Divine acting upon the physical being/body as the symbiotic relationship between spirit and matter

▲ Helps to attain inner peace and harmony with oneself; fosters greatness of soul and the desire to devote life to the service of the Divine/Higher Principles, despite disapproval from the outer world

INVERSIONS

▼ Causes adepts and others with spiritual power to become advocates for destructive, elitist, or exclusionary principles that would allocate love and forgiveness for some and not others

▼ Tendency to waste power and purpose on trivial concerns or causes, causing inner pollution and stagnation as well as ineffective actions

▼ Tendency to be consumed by internal warring and self-persecution that can cause depression, anxiety, and other psychological and physical maladies

▼ Corrupts apostates to become renegades and "rogues" who dishonor a mission, enterprise, group, or religion by scandalous behavior

42 Mikael

(MI-ka-EL)   *Political Authority and Order* (R)

Angel's Sign/Planet:	Sephira/Ruling Planet:	Choir/Archangel:
Libra/Saturn	Tiphareth/Sun	Virtues/Raphael

Incarnation Days:	Heart Days:	Intellect Time:
10/19–23	5/2, 7/16, 9/29, 12/10, 2/18	1:40–2:00 P.M.

VIRTUES

▲ Helps to incorporate the laws and hierarchy of Heaven (above) upon Earth (below) through motives and actions of individuals, society, and organizations

▲ Helps to align internal order so that the soul's purposes are implanted in the mind, carried out by the heart, and ultimately embodied on the physical plane

▲ Helps to work toward a perfect political order in which mankind can govern itself without need of police, military, or parliaments, and individuals can exercise their unique talents and aptitudes in alignment with his/her soul's purpose

▲ Helps to reconfigure and correct order on all levels; exposes conspiracies, treason, usurpers

▲ Helps to ensure a safe and expedient "voyage of life," so that emotional tendencies and passions do not disorient or cast one adrift into chaos

▲ Influences monarchs and heads of state, hierarchical obedience, duties, loyalty; helps to encourage leadership in politics/government and private enterprise toward noble purposes

INVERSIONS

▼ Tendency for communication with the Divine to be interrupted, distorted, or diluted so that the political order within individuals, religious societies, churches, etc., loses essence and becomes a pantomime

▼ Engenders malevolence, propaganda, traitors, destructive partisanship, abuse, misappropriation or instability of power, and legalization of base activities

▼ Tendency for self-deception, betrayal, and inner chaos

▼ Possibility of accidents or mishaps during travel

43 Veuliah

(vay-OO-lee-AH)   *Prosperity* (R)

Angel's Sign/Planet:	Sephira/Ruling Planet:	Choir/Archangel:
Scorpio/Jupiter	Tiphareth/Sun	Virtues/Raphael
Incarnation Days:	**Heart Days:**	**Intellect Time:**
10/24–28	5/3, 7/17, 9/30, 12/11, 2/19	2:00–2:20 P.M.

VIRTUES

▲ Helps to bring fertility, fruition, and largesse to all endeavors without struggle or great effort; brings particular success, fortune, and well-being near forty-second to forty-third birthday

▲ Helps to vanquish external and internal tyranny, obsessions, compulsions, and disturbances that can diminish and enslave the Eternal Self to karma; helps to defeat and pardon misdeeds and negatives in self and others by encouraging merits and positives

▲ Influences peace, prosperity, and power of countries, kingdoms, and thrones in the outer world (commerce, politics, society, etc.), as well as the inner worlds that spawn them (comprehension and implementation of universal principles)

▲ Brings the inner confidence of a royal as well as success in actual or metaphorical military realms and battles between Good and Evil

▲ Brings recognition and reward for noble, altruistic, or generous actions

INVERSIONS

▼ Tendency toward struggle, self-sabotage, fruitless efforts, stagnation, and failure

▼ Bearer or recipient of discord, partisanship, divisiveness, and ruin

▼ Tendency to seek prosperity and power by illicit or artificial means

▼ Uses prosperity to intimidate and corrupt

44 Yelahiah

(yay-LAH-hee-YAH)   *Karmic Warrior* (R)

Angel's Sign/Planet:	Sephira/Ruling Planet:	Choir/Archangel:
Scorpio/Mars	Tiphareth/Sun	Virtues/Raphael

Incarnation Days:	Heart Days:	Intellect Time:
10/29–11/2	5/4, 7/18, 10/1, 12/12, 2/20	2:20–2:40 P.M.

VIRTUES

▲ Brings willingness, skill, and courage to do battle with adverse forces and situations resulting from past actions; helps to vanquish old karmic debt with honor and glory

▲ Encourages travel as a way of learning, which also reflects the inner journey of dissolving karmic debt and acquiring wisdom

▲ Protects and prevails against weapons, armies, violence, and injustice; helps to apply military skills and bravery inwardly to become a victorious inner warrior

▲ Fosters a desire for justice and the ability to obtain good legal representation and a favorable outcome in the judicial process

INVERSIONS

▼ Tendency to be burdened and hindered by past actions

▼ Inability or unwillingness to recognize, reconcile, and resolve karmic debt; therefore may repeat past encroachments, vindictiveness, or atrocities and accumulate more karmic debt

▼ Creates an environment of constant conflict with perceived enemies and adversaries and a tendency to do battle for fruitless, ignoble, and destructive causes

▼ Likelihood of defeat, imprisonment, etc., by judicial process

45 Sehaliah

(say-HA-lee-YAH)   *Motivation and Willfulness* (S)

Angel's Sign/Planet:	Sephira/Ruling Planet:	Choir/Archangel:
Scorpio/Sun	Tiphareth/Sun	Virtues/Raphael
Incarnation Days:	Heart Days:	Intellect Time:
11/3-7	5/5, 7/19, 10/2, 12/13, 2/21	2:40-3:00 P.M.

VIRTUES

▲ Helps to recover will from the rule of egoistic desires and rampant emotions, restoring it to higher purposes; brings resiliency and renewed energy and determination to surmount obstacles and continue moving forward

▲ Endows with an inward luminosity that burns away negativity, spitefulness, pride, or excess in order to reestablish equilibrium and higher consciousness

▲ Helps to bring abundant means and faculties to manifest higher purposes

▲ Governs vegetation, the effectiveness of medicinal plants and regulation of the four elements of nature: the fire that purifies and warms, the water that washes away obstructions and irrigates, the earth that nurtures and blossoms, and the air that disperses the seeds that perpetuate all life cycles

▲ Propels the motor (fire) of living things, which is the heart, and assures good health and healing through proper irrigation of blood and other vital fluids that support the physical body

▲ Helps to exert strong healing influence on others and a tendency toward professions in medicine, healing, and teaching

INVERSIONS

▼ Instigates excess and extreme atmospheric conditions—torrid heat, freezing, aridity and drought, and intense humidity and torrential rains

▼ Creates excess and extremes in bodily humors and causes incurable maladies

▼ Perpetrator or victim of arid and unproductive endeavors

46 Ariel

(AH-ree-EL) *Perceiver and Revealer* (G)

Angel's Sign/Planet:	Sephira/Ruling Planet:	Choir/Archangel:
Scorpio/Venus	Tiphareth/Sun	Virtues/Raphael

Incarnation Days:	Heart Days:	Intellect Time:
11/8–12	5/6, 7/20, 10/3, 12/14, 2/22	3:00–3:20 P.M.

VIRTUES

▲ Patron of lotteries: helps to discover the Divine mysteries and philosophical secrets hidden in one's consciousness that can reveal the workings of "chance" in order to change life orientation and bring worldly fortune

▲ Helps to become a transmitter/communicator/intermediary between Divine Thought, human desire, and worldly manifestation

▲ Helps to transmit dreams, intents, and designs from spiritual or inner "above" into physical reality "below" via presentation of clear and comprehensible concepts

▲ Helps to receive and understand guidance from the language of the Emotional Self as expressed through metaphors, symbols, dreams, and events in daily life

▲ Fosters strong and intuitive perception of people and actions and the ability to resolve the most difficult problem

▲ Helps to foster discretion, subtlety, gratitude, and modesty

▲ Helps to become a strong spirit, a "Lion of God"

INVERSIONS

▼ Distorted or false perceptions, understandings, and communications

▼ Weak mentality, pride, foolish behavior, incoherence, wastefulness, overconsultation with mediums

▼ Absurd or unfruitful endeavors and enterprises

▼ Troubled, ill-at-ease, spiritually sick with many unresolved problems

47 Asaliah

(a-SA-lee-YAH)   *Contemplation* (R)

Angel's Sign/Planet:	Sephira/Ruling Planet:	Choir/Archangel:
Scorpio/Mercury	Tiphareth/Sun	Virtues/Raphael
Incarnation Days:	Heart Days:	Intellect Time:
11/13–17	5/7, 7/21, 10/4, 12/15, 2/23	3:20–3:40 P.M.

VIRTUES

▲ Helps to elevate attention and awareness above the details of life in order to contemplate cosmic order, justice, truth, and one's place and purpose within the "Greater Scheme"

▲ Helps to reveal the Divine at work within the Human; helps to infuse daily life and interactions with eternal principles

▲ Helps to attract people who will play important roles in the unfolding of one's personal stories, dreams, and goals

▲ Helps to connect one's own visions with those of other people so that the higher works and purposes of Heaven on Earth might be multiplied and strengthened

▲ Helps to infuse creative endeavors with a passion for clarity, truth, knowledge, and the enthusiasm to manifest projects on the material plane that reflect these values

▲ Fosters an ability to be a messenger or teacher sharing "hidden" spiritual and symbolic knowledge that can elevate consciousness and purposes of others in both daily and "envisioned life"

▲ Fosters an uncanny ability to seemingly know others' thoughts at times; helps to develop strong intuition into a psychology for self and others

INVERSIONS

▼ Tendency toward confusion, isolation, or unfruitful relationships and unfair situations that leave one feeling overwhelmed and lost

▼ Tendency to pollute life's greater purposes with self-serving motives that exclude the goals and contributions of others

▼ Tendency to overvalue the high ideals of others while diminishing one's own role and importance, which can ultimately cause existential "ennui" and despair about the purpose of one's own existence

▼ Tendency to misconstrue the motives and actions of others because of lack of self-worth and thwarted intuition

48 Mihael

(MIH-a-EL)   *Fertility, Fruitfulness* (G)

Angel's Sign/Planet:	Sephira/Ruling Planet:	Choir/Archangel:
Scorpio/Moon	Tiphareth/Sun	Virtues/Raphael

Incarnation Days:	Heart Days:	Intellect Time:
11/18–22	5/8, 7/22, 10/5, 12/16, 2/24	3:40–4:00 P.M.

VIRTUES

▲ Governs fertility, conception, and birth on physical, spiritual, and metaphorical levels

▲ Propels desire plus will to manifest form: helps dreams and visions descend from the plane of desire into the material world

▲ Gives strong desire to accomplish many and diverse milestones, paths, works; since desire is the primordial "motor" of all actions in the material world and works are the spiritual and material "children" of desire—the more precise, pure, and intentional the desires, the more fruitful their tangible manifestations

▲ Governs conjugal harmony and fidelity and helps heal, reconcile, and preserve union between spouses and partners; also helps to restore harmony between the inner masculine and feminine in order to manifest balanced desires and great works

▲ Governs paths of Sun (exterior/masculine), and Moon (interior/feminine); encourages mutuality and reciprocal pleasures of love and harmony between masculine and feminine forces

▲ Helps to fertilize collaborations and partnerships with energies and personnel needed to bring ripening and fruition

INVERSIONS

▼ Infertility, sterility, nonproductivity in personal life; ineffective efforts, work, enterprises that either do not produce fruit or result in contaminated or "inedible" fruit

▼ Jealousy, discord, divorce, dissolution between spouses and partners; confusion and self-alienation that result from disharmony between inner masculine and feminine aspects

▼ Tendency to treat another or be treated as a temporary or mere object of satisfaction and base desires

SEPHIRA 7
Netzach

DIVINE QUALILTY
VICTORY
Independence, Leadership, Triumph

ANGELIC ORDER/CHOIR
PRINCIPALITIES

ARCHANGEL
HANIEL

HUMAN QUALITIES
Leadership, Confidence, Independence,
Winning, Dominating, Parenting

HUMAN BODY
RIGHT LEG/PELVIS

RULING PLANET
VENUS

COLOR
GREEN

ANGELS
49 VEHUEL—*Elevation, Grandeur*
50 DANIEL—*Eloquence*
51 HAHASIAH—*Universal Medicine*
52 IMAMIAH—*Expiation of Errors*
53 NANAEL—*Spiritual Communication*
54 NITHAEL—*Rejuvenation and Eternal Youth*
55 MEBAHIAH—*Intellectual Lucidity*
56 POYEL—*Fortune and Support*

49 Vehuel

(VAY-hoo-EL)   *Elevation, Grandeur* (R)

Angel's Sign/Planet:	Sephira/Ruling Planet:	Choir/Archangel:
Sagittarius/Uranus	Netzach/Venus	Principalities/Haniel

Incarnation Days:	Heart Days:	Intellect Time:
11/23–27	5/9, 7/23, 10/6, 12/17, 2/25	4:00–4:20 P.M.

VIRTUES

▲ First Angel of Principalities charged with creating the seed which manifests form; source of inspiration for writers, great writings, and new expressions of intellect

▲ Gives ascent and intellectual force to a path or work motivated by Love and Wisdom; enables the works of Heaven (higher impulses) to be implanted on Earth (lower planes of manifestation, the body)

▲ Helps to be inspired and inspire others to higher thought and a return to innocence by transcending desires, passions, and base instincts

▲ Instills the desire to praise, celebrate, and glorify God in order to reignite the spark of vitality between the Human and the Divine

▲ Aids interior development and external manifestation of all who distinguish themselves by their talents, virtues, and willingness to engage true wisdom

▲ Fosters sensitivity, generosity of soul, virtues, good deeds, and esteem of others

▲ Helps to imbue the intellect with love in order to create wisdom, which in turn fosters a natural sense of justice, diplomacy, and the ability to present ideas and solutions that result in harmony among all parties

▲ Nurtures the ability to uplift, enrich, and appreciate all

▲ Helps to succeed in fields of literature, diplomatic service, and jurisprudence

INVERSIONS

▼ Tendency toward egoistic behavior without principles; actions motivated by hatred (loss of love), and expressing hypocrisy (degradation of diplomacy), and negativity (inversion of higher realms and purposes)

▼ Propensity to write or traffic in literature inspired by base realms, impulses, hatred, egoism

▼ Tendency toward unjust, self-serving, unprincipled legislation or diplomacy

50 Daniel

(DA-nee-EL)   *Eloquence* (R)

Angel's Sign/Planet:	Sephira/Ruling Planet:	Choir/Archangel:
Sagittarius/Saturn	Netzach/Venus	Principalities/Haniel

Incarnation Days:	Heart Days:	Intellect Time:
11/28–12/2	5/10, 7/24, 10/7, 12/18, 2/26	4:20–4:40 P.M.

VIRTUES

▲ Represents the power of eloquent and clear expression to relieve severity and give dignity and perspective to life's situations and conditions

▲ Helps to invoke compassion, justice, and patronage through attractive, persuasive presentation of ideas, thoughts, and opinions

▲ Helps to evaluate and choose courses of action, cure indecision, and reorient self and others when lost or confused

▲ Helps to be compassionate toward oneself and defend against internal judges by revealing the role of external factors

▲ Helps to bring consolation through Divine compassion and mercy

▲ Helps to be industrious and active; fosters love of literature and ability to distinguish self with eloquence as an author, screenwriter, publisher, etc.

▲ Helps ambassadors, attorneys, and advocates appeal to authorities on behalf of others

INVERSIONS

▼ Tendency for episodes of confused, convoluted, or inappropriate communication; represents opposition and impossibility rather than advocacy and possibility

▼ Uses eloquence for personal gain by manipulating, cheating, deceiving, exploiting others

▼ Tendency to engage in relationships, situations, or business on a false and illicit basis, i.e., as a "con man/woman"

▼ Tendency for confusion, indecision, self-judgment, harshness, and inability to communicate ideas clearly or persuasively

51 Hahasiah

(ha-HA-see-YAH)   *Universal Medicine* (R)

Angel's Sign/Planet:	Sephira/Ruling Planet:	Choir/Archangel:
Sagittarius/Jupiter	Netzach/Venus	Principalities/Haniel

Incarnation Days:	Heart Days:	Intellect Time:
12/3–7	5/11, 7/25 + 26 A.M., 10/8, 12/19, 2/27	4:40–5:00 P.M.

VIRTUES

▲ Brings the universal knowledge that enables understanding and healing of original causes of physical, emotional, and societal maladies; helps to manifest an ability to heal self and others or the ability to find a true healer when needed

▲ Facilitates the fundamental truths that effect transformation, sometimes referred to as the secrets of the "Philosopher's Stone"

▲ Elevates the soul toward contemplation of the Divine and the mysteries of universal wisdom

▲ Influences abstract and natural sciences: alchemy, metaphysics, and studies of the animal, vegetable, and mineral kingdoms

▲ Helps to distinguish oneself in medicine for important discoveries and "miraculous" cures

INVERSIONS

▼ Tendency toward grandiosity and charlatanism or being duped by a charlatan

▼ Tendency to abuse the good faith of others and to perpetrate or be a victim of impossible and undeliverable promises, false hopes, and values

▼ Stagnation of health, inability to heal, or discover cause of malady

52 Imamiah

(ee-MA-mee-YAH)   *Expiation of Errors* (R)

Angel's Sign/Planet:	Sephira/Ruling Planet:	Choir/Archangel:
Sagittarius/Mars	Netzach/Venus	Principalities/Haniel

Incarnation Days:	Heart Days:	Intellect Time:
12/8-12	5/12, 7/26 P.M. + 27, 10/9, 12/20, 2/28 + 29	5:00–5:20 P.M.

VIRTUES

▲ Helps to correct mistakes or unproductive situations fostered by distorted personal, familial, or societal belief systems

▲ Helps to realign and redeem motives and actions to create peace and the highest good for self and others

▲ Helps to free emotions from past burdensome or negative elements (one's own and others), thereby changing the weight of the past by changing its present and future effect

▲ Helps to bear life's ongoing adversities with patience and courage, but always in the context of creating oneself anew—not as a survivor of past error and difficulty, but rather as a new person with a clean slate who no longer needs the past as a continual reference point

▲ Helps to regain lost liberty and become an unencumbered, "lightened" being who sees problems or difficulties as opportunities to hone abilities and skills

▲ Helps to instill strength, stamina, determination, and a strong sense of self with unlimited possibilities and potentials

INVERSIONS

▼ Tendency to be overcome by pride, misery, and malevolence

▼ Suffers difficult, debilitating circumstances as a result of unresolved past mistakes and negative encounters, events, or personal history

▼ In danger of buckling under the weight of karmic debt and debilitation

53 Nanael

(NA-na-EL)   *Spiritual Communication* (R)

Angel's Sign/Planet:	Sephira/Ruling Planet:	Choir/Archangel:
Sagittarius/Sun	Netzach/Venus	Principalities/Haniel

Incarnation Days:	Heart Days:	Intellect Time:
12/13–16	5/13, 7/28, 10/10, 12/21, 3/1	5:20–5:40 P.M.

VIRTUES

▲ Helps to accept one's humanity by internalizing the esoteric sciences, thereby elevating ordinary desires and comprehension without contrivance or guilt

▲ Fosters a love of philosophy and a desire for personal spirituality and harmony with the laws of nature

▲ Nurtures a meditative disposition and need for solitude and rest to create a private sacred space for the cultivation of wisdom

▲ Helps to develop the ability to bring ideas, ideals, and wisdom to others

▲ Helps to sublimate and transcend physical desires in order to embrace the teachings of higher (heart/mind/spirit) realms; influences ecclesiastical, legal, and teaching professions

INVERSIONS

▼ Fosters ignorance, error, disharmony, and maladies of body and soul

▼ Tendency to misdirect others or be misled, bringing detours and delays

▼ Tendency toward confusion, chaos, and difficulty with studying and learning

▼ Possibility to be ruled or degraded by overfocusing on physical desires

54 Nithael

(NIT-ha-EL)   *Rejuvenation and Eternal Youth* (S)

Angel's Sign/Planet:	Sephira/Ruling Planet:	Choir/Archangel:
Sagittarius/Venus	Netzach/Venus	Principalities/Haniel

Incarnation Days:	Heart Days:	Intellect Time:
12/17–21	5/14, 7/29, 10/11, 12/22, 3/2	5:40–6:00 P.M.

VIRTUES

▲ Helps to live by motives and purposes that are in harmony with cosmic laws in order to tap the eternal resources which rejuvenate and extend life

▲ Helps to purify erroneous thoughts and actions in order not to be susceptible to conditions that imprison and deplete

▲ Helps to protect and purify "inner monarchs" so that bodily systems and functions are driven by true means and purposes, thereby bringing stability and freedom from inner conflicts that can cause premature aging

▲ Fosters great leadership, power, talent, renown, and esteem for righteousness and eloquence of speech and writing

▲ Influences and protects kings, princes, presidents, popes, bishops, and other political and religious heads of state and leaders who personally embody and endeavor to establish principles aligned with cosmic law, human rights, and justice

INVERSIONS

▼ Tendency for precarious and ruinous affairs in business, political, and societal situations

▼ Suffers or causes illegitimate, fraudulent situations and relationships, loss of integrity, and reputation

▼ Usurps positions and purposes of others, or in danger of being usurped and disenfranchised

▼ Officiates at public functions and events without being prepared

55 Mebahiah

(Me-BA-hee-YAH)   *Intellectual Lucidity* (G)

Angel's Sign/Planet:	Sephira/Ruling Planet:	Choir/Archangel:
Capricorn/Mercury	Netzach/Venus	Principalities/Haniel

Incarnation Days:	Heart Days:	Intellect Time:
12/22–26	5/15, 7/30, 10/12, 12/23, 3/3	6:00–6:20 P.M.

VIRTUES

▲ Helps to use intelligence for the purposes of heart and soul rather than for the sake of intelligence only, thereby bringing the purposes of Heaven to Earth and giving what we create nobler value

▲ Helps to imbue intelligence with a love for truth, clarity, and fidelity to higher principles and ideals

▲ Helps to prepare the internal emotional and physical "intelligences" to receive the seeds of creation in order to perpetuate Divine Essence through human life, ideas, and ideals

▲ Helps to distinguish and employ the smallest details of information picked up by the five senses

▲ Brings consolation and higher intelligence to malady and sickness in order to plant seeds for healing

▲ Helps and protects those who work to advance and maintain the higher purposes of morality, religion, and altruism within themselves and in the external world

INVERSIONS

▼ Displays intellectual naïveté or conceit; uses intelligence for material gain and selfish, ignoble purposes

▼ Opposes truth, clarity, and morality; enemy of higher/spiritual/religious principles and ideals and those who strive to uphold them

▼ Difficulty in overcoming a malady or illness of body, mind, or enterprise

56 Poyel

(Poi-YEL)   *Fortune and Support* (G)

Angel's Sign/Planet:	Sephira/Ruling Planet:	Choir/Archangel:
Capricorn/Moon	Netzach/Venus	Principalities/Haniel

Incarnation Days:	Heart Days:	Intellect Time:
12/27–31	5/16, 7/31, 10/13, 12/24, 3/4	6:20–6:40 P.M.

VIRTUES

▲ Helps to generate timely good fortune, abundance, and fame through the workings of talent and humility

▲ Encourages modesty, moderation, and agreeableness, which helps to use power and stature respectfully, thereby earning the esteem of others

▲ Helps to form images (film, photography, sculpture, painting) that express clarity, power, and a philosophy for "the people" that is simple and accessible rather than complex or scholarly

▲ Helps to receive support from a mentor or benefactor and/or willingness to guide and support others

INVERSIONS

▼ Tendency to be ambitious, arrogant, presumptuous, authoritative, and dominated by pride

▼ Pretentious and self-elevating at the expense or exclusion of others

▼ Causes or suffers deprivation or hoarding and stagnation of fortune

Hod

DIVINE QUALILTY
GLORY/SPLENDOR
Dependence, Surrender

ANGELIC ORDER/CHOIR
ARCHANGELS

ARCHANGEL
MIKHAEL

HUMAN QUALITY
Interdependence and vulnerability that fosters collaboration
for a greater combined outcome

HUMAN BODY
LEFT LEG/PELVIS

RULING PLANET
MERCURY

COLOR
ORANGE

ANGELS
57 NEMAMIAH—*Discernment*
58 YEIALEL—*Mental Force*
59 HARAHEL—*Intellectual Richness*
60 MITZRAEL—*Internal Reparation*
61 UMABEL—*Affinity and Friendship*
62 IAH-HEL—*Desire to Know*
63 ANAUEL—*Perception of Unity*
64 MEHIEL—*Vivification (Invigorate, Enliven)*

57 Nemamiah

(ne-MA-mee-YAH)   *Discernment* (R)

Angel's Sign/Planet:	Sephira/Ruling Planet:	Choir/Archangel:
Capricorn/Uranus	Hod/Mercury	Archangels/Mikhael

Incarnation Days:	Heart Days:	Intellect Time:
1/1–5	5/17, 8/1, 10/14, 12/25, 3/5	6:40–7:00 P.M.

VIRTUES

▲ Helps to avoid or correct errors, confusions, and inconsistencies in stories and scenarios of life

▲ Helps to develop understanding and appropriate response to current situations; helps to discern people and influences opposed to needs and interests

▲ Brings prosperity in all things due to mental clarity and astuteness

▲ Helps to win outer-world victory that mirrors victory in intellectual combat and the "war within"; helps to combat fatigue with courage and productive activity

▲ Fosters a propensity for the avant-garde and to be a forerunner

▲ Aids captains, generals, and all who fight for just causes; helps to know the precise moment of advantage for victory

INVERSIONS

▼ Lack of clarity or misinterpretation of underlying issues or the bigger picture; tendency to mislead others or be misled by passions, false information, or misunderstandings

▼ Indecisive, hesitant, prisoner of inertia or routine, chronic health complaints

▼ Mistreatment of those who are vulnerable and defenseless; tendency for self-sabotage and defeat

58 Yeialel

(YAY-a-LEL)   *Mental Force* (R)

Angel's Sign/Planet:	Sephira/Ruling Planet:	Choir/Archangel:
Capricorn/Saturn	Hod/Mercury	Archangels/Mikhael

Incarnation Days:	Heart Days:	Intellect Time:
1/6–10	5/18, 8/2, 10/15, 12/26, 3/6	7:00–7:20 P.M.

VIRTUES

▲ Helps to master emotions and impulses and to focus on what is essential, logical, and just, thereby aligning actions with Divine Laws and accelerating evolvement

▲ Helps to heal maladies (caused by excess or distortions of emotions), particularly disturbances of the eyes, which symbolize perception and clarity

▲ Encourages bravery and the clarity to defend against internal and external enemies, false witnesses, injustice, and corruption

▲ Helps to uproot the bad seed and "separate the wheat from the chaff"

▲ Fosters intensity, purity, truth, clarity, and love in the highest sense, feelings and forms

INVERSIONS

▼ Prone to anger, irritability, moroseness, pessimism, and weakness of mentality due to distorted emotions and impulses

▼ Tends toward violence and revenge at the least provocation

▼ Perpetrates or is victim of homicide, assassination, unjust war

59 Harahel

(HA-ra-HEL)   *Intellectual Richness* (R)

Angel's Sign/Planet:	Sephira/Ruling Planet:	Choir/Archangel:
Capricorn/Jupiter	Hod/Mercury	Archangels/Mikhael

Incarnation Days:	Heart Days:	Intellect Time:
1/11–15	5/19 + 20 A.M., 8/3, 10/16, 12/27 A.M., 3/7	7:20–7:40 P.M.

VIRTUES

▲ Represents remarkable practical/worldly intelligence with the ability to manifest spirituality in worldly constructions

▲ Helps to administer public funds and manage financial speculations, investments, enterprises, and fortunes

▲ Assists the ability to learn and/or teach easily and to utilize intellectual faculties to attain the treasures of life

▲ Supports female fertility, helps with problems of sterility

▲ Encourages respect and understanding between parents and children

▲ Brings success in printing and publishing business, bookstores, writing, journalism, sciences, commerce, finance, music, world affairs, and human relations

INVERSIONS

▼ Mental opacity, dullness, or aberration

▼ Enemy of light, ruin, and destruction by fire

▼ Involvement in fraudulent banking or embezzlement

▼ Tends toward unsuccessful enterprises, failed world endeavors, and sterility on all levels

60 Mitzrael

(MITS-ra-EL)   *Internal Reparation* (R)

Angel's Sign/Planet:	Sephira/Ruling Planet:	Choir/Archangel:
Capricorn/Mars	Hod/Mercury	Archangels/Mikhael

Incarnation Days:	Heart Days:	Intellect Time:
1/16–20	5/20 P.M. + 21, 8/4, 10/17, 12/27 P.M., 3/8	7:40–8:00 P.M.

VIRTUES

▲ Helps to repair the conduits of communication between the soul and the body in order to rehabilitate destructive emotions and passions; helps to triumph over internal and external enemies and persecutors

▲ Helps to develop high morals, loyalty, and obedience to superiors

▲ Fosters good health and longevity

▲ Helps to become a great healer of mental maladies, such as a psychiatrist, psychologist, therapist, or analyst

INVERSIONS

▼ Displays insubordination, revolt, disloyalty, disobedience: rebellion against parents, laws, ideologies, principles, and civil or military powers

▼ Propensity for sickness, depression, mental illness, short life

▼ Tendency for contaminated and short-lived enterprises

61 Umabel

(OO-ma-BEL)   *Affinity and Friendship* (R)

Angel's Sign/Planet:	Sephira/Ruling Planet:	Choir/Archangel:
Aquarius/Sun	Hod/Mercury	Archangels/Mikhael

Incarnation Days:	Heart Days:	Intellect Time:
1/21–25	5/22, 8/5, 10/18, 12/28, 3/9	8:00–8:20 P.M.

VIRTUES

▲ Instills an understanding of the essential affinity between Heaven and Earth and the vital importance of collaboration between all things above and below

▲ Helps to develop the intellect to perceive the essential natures of life-forms in the vegetable, mineral, animal, and human kingdoms—as well as understand the influences of shared affinities and connectedness in form and function

▲ Helps to discover secrets of the natural world and to develop knowledge of herbs and other substances that may be used for medicinal and healing purposes

▲ Helps to discover methods and means for creating or maintaining affinities between seemingly disparate elements, situations, domains, philosophies, or peoples

▲ Fosters a love of voyages, journeys, and enjoyment of diverse peoples and friendships that may even surpass the need for partner love

▲ Helps to develop communication and liaisons with many like-minded people for friendship or shared interests and professions; helps to work interdependently with others toward shared goals

▲ Encourages interest in sciences that involve correspondences, particularly physics, chemistry, astronomy, and astrology

INVERSIONS

▼ Tendency to be adrift, scattered, chaotic, and friendless, with no accountability for behavior

▼ Opposes the natural order of things, situations, people, values, and life

▼ Suffers disturbance of internal natural order, causing susceptibility to diseases that cause the body to fight itself, such as immune system disorders

▼ Uses knowledge and connectedness for insincere or illicit motives and self-interest

62 Iah-hel

(EE-a-HEL)   *Desire to Know* (R)

Angel's Sign/Planet:	Sephira/Ruling Planet:	Choir/Archangel:
Aquarius/Venus	Hod/Mercury	Archangels/Mikhael
Incarnation Days:	Heart Days:	Intellect Time:
1/26–30	5/23, 8/6, 10/19, 12/29, 3/10	8:20–8:40 P.M.

VIRTUES

▲ Encourages toward the road less traveled and productive disengagement from the material world in favor of adventures that bring knowledge

▲ Helps to understand the "world of creation" on the deepest and highest levels; helps to search for understanding of cause and effect in daily life and conditions

▲ Inspires the philosopher and mystic: helps guide the descent of knowledge from the mind into the heart, where knowledge is transformed into wisdom and understanding

▲ Fosters love of tranquility and solitude in order to receive illumination and knowledge from within

▲ Helps to fulfill duties and obligations and to be distinguished by virtue and modesty

INVERSIONS

▼ Tendency toward inconstancy, restlessness, and shallow uses of deeper subjects such as philosophy and spirituality

▼ Search for luxury, pleasures; inconsequential use of time, associations, and communication

▼ Prone to unfaithfulness, disloyalties, scandals, rifts, and divorce between masculine and feminine

63 Anauel

(a-NA-oo-EL)   *Perception of Unity* (S)

Angel's Sign/Planet:	Sephira/Ruling Planet:	Choir/Archangel:
Aquarius/Mercury	Hod/Mercury	Archangels/Mikhael

Incarnation Days:	Heart Days:	Intellect Time:
1/31–2/4	5/24, 8/7, 10/20, 12/30, 3/11	8:40–9:00 P.M.

VIRTUES

▲ Helps to be freed of excessive pride and bias of race and culture in order to see all people as citizens and coparticipants of community, Earth and the universe

▲ Helps to transcend emotional dependencies and preferences to enter into a universal sense of connectedness

▲ Establishes communication and unity between inner and outer worlds; helps to bring wisdom and spiritual values to the individual as well as to the global community and abolishes old beliefs that divide and alienate

▲ Helps to cultivate and express remarkable practical intelligence and reason

▲ Protects against accidents, guards health, and fights maladies caused by overindulgence of emotions and desires

▲ Helps to bring great success in business, commerce, banking, and industry

INVERSIONS

▼ Self-alienation, isolation, elitism, and disconnectedness from others

▼ Lacking in common sense, reason, practicality; inability to control desires and urges

▼ Misdirected and poor business affairs ending in ruin and loss

▼ Propensity for paralysis and stagnation of efforts or results

64 Mehiel

(MAY-hee-EL)   *Vivification (Invigorate, Enliven)* (G)

Angel's Sign/Planet:	Sephira/Ruling Planet:	Choir/Archangel:
Aquarius/Moon	Hod/Mercury	Archangels/Mikhael

Incarnation Days:	Heart Days:	Intellect Time:
2/5–9	5/25, 8/8, 10/21, 12/31, 3/12	9:00–9:20 P.M.

VIRTUES

▲ Helps to quicken thoughts and ideas into material reality through passion, commitment, and determination

▲ Helps to assemble and coordinate expert allies and collaborators to complete a job in the most fruitful and productive means possible

▲ Helps to bring timeliness and other elements of advantage to plans and points of action

▲ Influences and helps to bring success to authors and storytellers, orators, actors, professors, philosophers, publishers, booksellers, and other commerce relating to literature and the dissemination of ideas

INVERSIONS

▼ Tendency to construct hollow, nonsubstantive, or unfounded works

▼ Tendency for unfruitful enterprises that lack the vitality to continue or to be resurrected

▼ Tendency to be lax and unmotivated or a pseudo-expert and plagiarist of the ideas and works of others

Yesod

DIVINE QUALILTY
FOUNDATION
Interdependence—Balances Independence and Dependence

ANGELIC ORDER/CHOIR
ANGELS-CHERUBS

ARCHANGEL
GABRIEL

HUMAN QUALITIES
Dance of interdependence between male and female
and all versions of duality that enable the forms of life
to be created and perpetuated

HUMAN BODY
SEXUAL ORGANS

RULING PLANET
MOON

COLOR
PURPLE

ANGELS
65 DAMABIAH—*Fountain of Wisdom*
66 MANAKEL—*Knowledge of Good and Evil*
67 EYAEL—*Transformation to the Sublime*
68 HABUHIAH—*Healing*
69 ROCHEL—*Restitution*
70 JABAMIAH—*Alchemy (Transformation)*
71 HAIYAEL—*Divine Warrior/Weaponry*
72 MUMIAH—*Endings and Rebirth*

65 Damabiah

(da-MA-bee-YAH)   *Fountain of Wisdom* (R)

Angel's Sign/Planet:	Sephira/Ruling Planet:	Choir/Archangel:
Aquarius/Uranus	Yesod/Moon	Angels-Cherubs/Gabriel

Incarnation Days:	Heart Days:	Intellect Time:
2/10–14	5/26, 8/9, 10/22, 1/1, 3/13	9:20–9:40 P.M.

VIRTUES

▲ Helps to receive and distill wisdom from above so that it might be manifested in the motives and machinations of earthly endeavors

▲ Helps to develop enterprises that embody and expand the application of higher principles

▲ Fosters the wisdom necessary to formulate and implement positive solutions

▲ Helps to channel wisdom to the emotions (water) through intuition; brings vitality and rejuvenation to all aspects of earthly life through the cleansing circulation of emotions

▲ Influences human endeavors involving water, particularly naval and maritime expeditions, commercial enterprises, construction, and personnel

▲ Helps to develop an inner richness and generosity that spills over into the external world as material fortune

INVERSIONS

▼ Provokes or becomes a victim of climactic (outer) or emotional (inner) tempests and floods; brings chaos, contradiction, and confusion of ideas and emotions that can cause tumult and aggression

▼ Tendency for ineffective, failed enterprises and endeavors

▼ Propensity for shallow liaisons and multiple casual affairs

▼ Suffers excess or stagnation of bodily humors

66 Manakel

(MA-na-KEL)   *Knowledge of Good and Evil* (R)

Angel's Sign/Planet:	Sephira/Ruling Planet:	Choir/Archangel:
Aquarius/Saturn	Yesod/Moon	Angels-Cherubs/Gabriel

Incarnation Days:	Heart Days:	Intellect Time:
2/15–19	5/27, 8/10, 10/23, 1/2, 3/14	9:40–10:00 P.M.

VIRTUES

▲ Gives the capacity to discern whether encounters, events, or enterprises will be positive or negative before they are undertaken; helps to develop an internal "voice" that acts to get our attention and to inform and protect against naïveté, ignorance, or error

▲ Helps to dampen and transform potentially destructive and consuming forces of internal and external fire so that they can be used as creative energies

▲ Helps to understand the presence of "Evil" as inversions of positive qualities and energies resulting from polluted and out-of-balance conditions or systems (note that "evil" spells "live" backward)

▲ Helps to use symptoms of negative conditions or forces as indications for the need to clean, cure, and purify in order to restore equilibrium and positive energy

▲ Helps to build high moral character and construct one's inner temple with elements that can withstand internal and external "demons" of destruction

▲ Helps to use dreams as an avenue for heightened awareness and guidance for success in daily endeavors and choices

▲ Influences vegetation, irrigation, and aquatic animals; supports the life-affirming flora and fauna of our own internal terrain and sea of emotions in order to maintain harmony of body and soul

INVERSIONS

▼ Tendency to be without principle or morality and to use relationships and situations for malignant and selfish material interests

▼ Tendency to manifest disease and to exhibit external physical appearance as reflection of corrupted values, inner "demons," and arid, polluted internal environment

▼ Susceptibility to corrupt and distort use of spiritual principles or to be a victim or practitioner of "black magic"

67 Eyael

(AY-ya-EL)   *Transformation to the Sublime* (R)

Angel's Sign/Planet:	Sephira/Ruling Planet:	Choir/Archangel:
Pisces/Jupiter	Yesod/Moon	Angels-Cherubs/Gabriel

Incarnation Days:	Heart Days:	Intellect Time:
2/20–24	5/28, 8/11, 10/24, 1/3, 3/15	10:00–10:20 P.M.

VIRTUES

▲ Helps to detect origins (the initial state of things) and discern how to transform one substance into another in order to elevate and expand its life-affirming elements

▲ Helps to perceive and transform abstract truths into concrete truths that may be manifested in constructive works

▲ Helps to purify emotions so that feelings and motives are informed by the highest principles

▲ Helps to maintain composure and inner ballast in the face of adversity

▲ Influences love of solitude, contemplation, and meditation

▲ Influences toward abstract and higher sciences such as philosophy, physics, astronomy, astrology, alchemy, and the Kabbalah

INVERSIONS

▼ Exhibits biases, mistaken perceptions, errors in judgment, and ill-informed actions

▼ Tendency toward conformist thinking or to become a "false" prophet or proclaimer without morals or principles

▼ Easily derailed and demoted, difficulty being alone, haunted by impure feelings and thoughts

68 Habuhiah

(ha-BU-hee-YAH)   *Healing* (R)

Angel's Sign/Planet:	Sephira/Ruling Planet:	Choir/Archangel:
Pisces/Mars	Yesod/Moon	Angels-Cherubs/Gabriel

Incarnation Days:	Heart Days:	Intellect Time:
2/25–29	5/29, 8/12, 10/25, 1/4, 3/16	10:20–10:40 P.M.

VIRTUES

▲ Helps to cure or be cured of maladies quickly in order to return to and maintain good health

▲ Helps to return to harmony with Divine standards and principles (as in the story of "the Prodigal Son")

▲ Helps to overcome the "beasts within" to regulate desires and animalistic tendencies that disrupt mental and emotional health

▲ Helps to correct and heal discrepancies and misalignments that occur within the self as well as in external relationships and situations

▲ Brings a love of nature, countryside, open spaces, farming and agricultural life, as well as an ability to receive healing energies from the natural world

▲ Helps to cultivate a fertile, hardworking nature with great creative power

INVERSIONS

▼ Predisposition for infections, contagions, multiple maladies, and chronic conditions

▼ Sterility of nature, unyielding agriculture, famine, and pestilence

▼ Cut off from cosmic nourishment; stagnation of feelings and ideas that ultimately cause inner pollution and misery

69 Rochel

(ro-SHEL)   *Restitution* (R)

Angel's Sign/Planet:	Sephira/Ruling Planet:	Choir/Archangel:
Pisces/Sun	Yesod/Moon	Angels-Cherubs/Gabriel

Incarnation Days:	Heart Days:	Intellect Time:
3/1–5	5/30, 8/13, 10/26, 1/5, 3/17	10:40–11:00 P.M.

VIRTUES

▲ Helps to recover lost or stolen objects and discover the perpetrator, as well as to understand the karmic relationship and reasons for the theft/loss; fosters the humility to correct wrongful actions and to return or attribute to others what belongs to them

▲ Helps to recover the divine self that is one's birthright: reunites lower and higher consciousness and nurtures an inner androgyny that embraces both genders and is restricted by neither

▲ Helps to discover truth through the path of intuition

▲ Helps to walk the way of "Ariadne's Thread" by following the thread of love that connects and reunites relationships through "going the distance" and conquering the "demons" within; helps to reunite the one with the many via the unforeseen and coincidental

▲ Helps to ensure right motivation and use of innate talents, skills, and potential, thereby maximizing positive influence on others

▲ Instills an interest to explore the ways and customs of other cultures, laws, peoples, etc.

▲ Brings inheritance, favor, fame, fortune, and success

▲ Bestows judiciousness and influences advocates, lawyers, and legalities

INVERSIONS

▼ Suffers or commits theft, ruin, disinheritance

▼ Exhibits wrong use of talents and skills, distorted motivations and intuitions, and perpetuation of negativity

▼ Brings or suffers lawsuits, poor advocacy, adverse judgments, and injustice

▼ Tendency to be lost, confused, and undermined by inner "demons"

70 Jabamiah

(ya-BA-mee-YAH)   *Alchemy (Transformation)* (R)

Angel's Sign/Planet:	Sephira/Ruling Planet:	Choir/Archangel:
Pisces/Venus	Yesod/Moon	Angels-Cherubs/Gabriel

Incarnation Days:	Heart Days:	Intellect Time:
3/6–10	5/31, 8/14, 10/27, 1/6, 3/18	11:00–11:20 P.M.

VIRTUES

▲ Represents the "Great Alchemist": Helps to turn the base mettle of human substance into spiritual gold by transforming instincts, impulses, and tendencies into golden thoughts, feelings, and deeds

▲ Helps to bring Heaven to Earth by manifesting and embodying higher/Divine Principles on the earthly plane, so that "as it is above, so it is below"

▲ Helps to purify and ennoble the temple of the body and altar of the heart so that the highest creative forces may be received and utilized

▲ Helps to procreate, regenerate, and revitalize, bringing fertility and abundance to all endeavors

▲ Gives power of healing, even in cases abandoned by medical profession

▲ Helps to transform society with ideas and ideals

▲ Helps to become a great thinker, philosophical light, lover of Truth, sage, and teacher

INVERSIONS

▼ Destruction of natural world and inner nature in search of material earthly gold

▼ Tendency for riches and success to be despoiled, squandered, and depleted

▼ Engages in downside of capitalism: tendency to exploit ideas and ideals for personal gain at the expense of others

▼ Tendency toward opportunistic atheism, promoting/exploiting different sects for acquisition of money and power

▼ Initiates literary disputes and criticism

▼ Tendency for incurable disease

71 Haiyael

(HA-ee-ya-EL)   *Divine Warrior/Weaponry* (R)

Angel's Sign/Planet:	Sephira/Ruling Planet:	Choir/Archangel:
Pisces/Mercury	Yesod/Moon	Angels-Cherubs/Gabriel

Incarnation Days:	Heart Days:	Intellect Time:
3/11–15	6/1, 8/15, 10/28, 1/7, 3/19	11:20–11:40 P.M.

VIRTUES

▲ Provides inner weaponry for protection (shield) and discernment (sword) to manifest victory and peace on spiritual and worldly planes

▲ Brings vitality, courage, creativity, and clarity to help storm the inner and outer citadels and vanquish external tyrants, which are often the mirrors of inner saboteurs

▲ Helps to ennoble and strengthen the emotions and to engender loyalty, bravery, and courage for just causes

▲ Cultivates heroic military genius that reestablishes authentic order and unity in the inner worlds of feelings and ideas and the outer worlds of society and its systems

▲ Helps to transform an internal "Babylon" of chaos to a "New Jerusalem" of order, harmony, and peaceful existence with ourselves and others

INVERSIONS

▼ Uses arms to advance motives of lower impulses such as selfishness, greed, or pride

▼ Expresses discordant opposing interests in relationships, partnerships, and ventures that can result in rupture

▼ Causes disturbance of inner/outer order that can ultimately lead to criminal activities

▼ Exhibits excessive and staunch rationality

▼ Tendency for disloyalty and betrayal of self and others

72 Mumiah

(MOO-mee-YAH)   *Endings and Rebirth* (S)

Angel's Sign/Planet:	Sephira/Ruling Planet:	Choir/Archangel:
Pisces/Moon	Yesod/Moon	Angels-Cherubs/Gabriel

Incarnation Days:	Heart Days:	Intellect Time:
3/16 - 20	6/2, 8/16, 10/29, 1/8, 3/20	11:40 - 12:00 A.M.

VIRTUES

▲ Helps to complete a cycle or phase and carries seed for rebirth, vitality, and new beginnings

▲ Helps to instill hope and future fertility by bringing an end to a period of misery, illness, difficulties, desperation, and oppression—which may manifest individually as the end of a relationship, job, particular life circumstances, or life itself; globally this could mean the end of a government regime, natural technological cataclysms, eradication of territorial boundaries or other life forms and systems

▲ Encourages the right use of medicine to bring about extraordinary cures and longevity; helps to understand the metaphors of illness for healing and undergo a transformation of biochemistry, if necessary, for a complete return to health

▲ Helps to use adversity and difficulty as an opportunity for discovery and success

▲ Helps to heal grief from loss or death by nurturing the potential for new life

▲ Influences professions in medical fields and extraordinary work in the curative properties of nature, biochemistry, health, and longevity

INVERSIONS

▼ Sees horizons as bleak and black, life as merely the anteroom to death, and endings as finalities without hope or opportunity

▼ Tendency toward loss and inability to prosper in health, love, friendship, work, or fortune

▼ Despairing, detesting one's own existence, suicidal or death wish that may be fulfilled through accident or sickness

SEPHIRA 10
Malkuth

also called SHEKINAH

DIVINE QUALILTY
CREATION/HUMANKIND
Kingdom of Heaven on Earth

ANGELIC ORDER/CHOIR
(No Angels in this Sephira)
REALM OF SAINTS AND BEATIFIED SOULS

ARCHANGEL
URIEL/SANDALPHON

HUMAN QUALITIES
Physical manifestation, completion of projects
and all forms of creativity, created things, and beings

HUMAN BODY
WHOLE BODY/WOMAN

RULING PLANET
EARTH

COLOR
SPECTRUM OF ALL COLORS OR SKY BLUE

4.

HEART, WING, AND A PRAYER—TOOLS FOR TRANSFORMATION

The Three-step Angel path of change

Not only do the 72 Angels transform us by "downloading" Divine Energy within us, but they also change the very substance of our being by enhancing our awareness and raising our consciousness. The Angels, therefore, act as "alchemical" agents of change within us and can enhance our lives on every level of expression and experience.

The principles of alchemy are very much present in the 72 Angels tradition. As mentioned in chapter 2, footnote 1, alchemy is concerned with transformational change (see also chapter 9 for a brief origin and history of alchemy). A syllabic analysis of transformation—formation that goes "across" or "beyond" form—implies something deeper than change of appearance, attitude, time, or place. Transformation involves *reconfiguration* of thought, action, and/or being, and it can alter radically the way we are affected by our life experiences. When transformational work aims at healing and recovery, the results can far surpass those of traditional therapeutic methods. For example, psychotherapy can show us how to survive painful events and their memories; transformation, on the other hand, can substantially *erase* a history of pain and create us anew. Transformation is not something we can rationalize, analyze, or force our way through. It is something that must be allowed by a willing and malleable heart. The heart—our existential and emotional hub, our most private and intimate part—is where the Angels do their most profound transformational work.

As Gail Godwin explores in her book entitled *Heart*, almost every mystical system in the history of the world tells us that we can come to know the mind of the Divine through the medium of our hearts, and it is here where our most potent communication with the Divine occurs—for example, the fervent prayer. In Hindu mysticism, the Upanishads (meaning "connection") "focus[es] on the God to be discovered [where it] already resides in the secret cave of our heart . . . the great fulcrum of the cosmos" (p. 43). Aryeh Kaplan suggests in his commentary on the *Sefer Yetzirah* that "it is in the heart that the action of [Divine] Mind is manifest in the body . . . and the heart serves as a causal link between mind and body . . . Therefore . . . the power of perception and the soul's ability to nourish itself must lie in the heart" (p. 76). Time and again, healing methods have shown that when the heart is opened—awakened—transformed—all other aspects of ourselves begin to heal.

Siddha Yoga guru Bagwan Nitchananda said, "The heart is the hub of all sacred places." There is no search for purpose and meaning more relevant to our particular desires, dreams, and challenges than what takes place in the intimacy of our individual hearts. Ironically, however, our heart is often held at the greatest distance from our choices and life paths. Jay Ramsay says in *Alchemy—The Art of Transformation*, "Your heart is the wound and your heart is the key" (p. 130, ibid.). Although the pain of a broken heart can be almost unbearable, we have only to tap deep into the reservoir of our hearts to receive the infinite power of healing and reenlivening that awaits us there.

The Three-step Angel path

If we can find the courage to cross our threshold of resistance and self-protection into the yearning of our hearts, the Angels will meet us there. *The ability to empower ourselves begins with the willingness and humility to ask*—to "call down" the Divine to that most intimate, personally relevant place. It is here in our hearts where we may communicate with the Divine without reservations or boundaries—and where profound and lasting change can occur.

The practical work of the Kabbalah is based on the premise that the nature and desire of the Divine to give is triggered by humanity's desire and willingness to receive. The sacred mysteries claim that when we invoke, pray, or ask something of the Divine, the Angels act as "amplifiers." They relay our request and bring back a response in an accessible, receivable form.

We can put the transformative dynamic of the Angels into play by working daily with our Birth Angels or any of the other 72 Angels in a continual three-step path that invites us to:

1. **Invoke:** pray/chant/speak the Angel's name and *ask* for its Presence
2. **Imbibe:** hear/breathe in/meditate upon and *receive* the Angel's essence and energy
3. **Embody:** absorb/digest/assimilate/*become* the Angel's quality

Engaging with the Angels is a "come as you are" adventure. You don't have to be a different or better person, know theological doctrine, or obtain anyone's permission or absolution to pray, chant, meditate, or ask for help. The Angelic Energies do not ask for ritual or prostration, nor must you earn their favor by proselytizing or defending their sacredness to others. Furthermore, total comprehension of this or any other book is not necessary—whenever you call the Angels, they will begin to work within you. All you need is a willingness within yourself for them to appear. Ask for their presence and receive them with your heart, mind, and body.

The Angels can reveal the fullness of who you already are and what paths and purposes in the world truly belong to you. No two people experience the Divine in the same way. The nature of your relationship with the Angels will be an intimacy between you and them that can never be dictated or known by any other. Through daily attention and practice, you may engage in a deeply personal relationship with the Angels that will enable you to take in and utilize the Divine qualities they embody in a way that is most relevant to your own qualities and concerns.

Let's explore in details the three steps that engage the Angels in our lives. Note that each step is vitally intertwined with elements of the other two steps.

1. Invoking—Asking for an Angel's Attention, Presence, and Help

By *invoking* an Angel's name and "person" with focused intent, we invite them within and activate their ability to engage with us. When we ask for what we truly desire, we "draw down" more and more Divine Fullness into this earthly plane. Invoking, praying, and calling upon the Angelic representatives of the Divine are humble acts that connect us to boundless empowerment. As Ramsay says in *Alchemy*, "The power of prayer lies in its ability to soften and attune us . . . [which is] related to receptivity" (p. 53, ibid.). If we relinquish the need to have total control, we can collaborate with the Angels in the further creation and fulfillment of ourselves. Ultimately, we will be of greater service to others through a continuing ability to siphon the Divine Essence and Energies of love and unlimitedness.

How to Ask. An Angel's name represents a vibratory aspect of the Divine that is both quantitative and qualitative (see chapter 1). When we speak its name we invite the energetic charge held in the name to emit its qualities in response. By invoking the Angels in this way, we focus our own awareness and give them permission— by the acquiescence of our free will—to engage with us.

To prepare yourself to ask, it might be helpful to clear and calm your presence of any disturbing or negative energies. But remember, *the Divine receives us as who we are, not who we might think we should be.* By asking from where and who we are in the moment, we unleash the power of the Angels to help us move beyond present circumstances and limitations into a more powerfully endowed future. If you are in distress, acknowledge that fact or feeling and ask for what you need—the Angels will respond.

To invoke a specific Angel, speak or chant the Angel's name while praying or meditating. Invite a feeling of the Angel's presence to inhabit you. In addition, speaking aloud to the Angels or any aspect of the Divine can enable you to relate immediately to your emotions, confusions, or frustrations. Speaking aloud also compels you to focus and clarify your thoughts. Suddenly, you may understand what you really want, and perhaps what inner or outer obstacles are preventing you from obtaining your goals.

The Angels help us to know and do *what we truly desire.* So when you ask for their help, do not ask them to supplant your own will, but to purify it so you can become aligned with your true potential. Your deepest, truest urges are clues to the Divine blueprint for your particular life. The Angels come to assist us, and they thrive on our willingness to do what we truly envision for our lives. In my own life, during a time of making difficult decisions about changes in career direction I asked again and again, "What should I do?" The answer was always, "What do YOU WANT to do?" or "Decide where YOU want to go, and we will help you get there"—and simply, "Follow your heart, and your feet will know where to go!" As Robert Fritz said in *The Path of Least Resistance*, sometimes we limit our dreams by what circumstances, other people or our own fears have made us think is impossible. As soon as I stopped thinking about the obstacles and started to focus on a destination—and take a first step—"help" seemed to be unleashed from everywhere.

There is a deeper aspect involved in asking that healers, energy practitioners, "positive thinkers," and others say creates the most tangible results. In its simplest form, it involves *believing* without a doubt that we can, and will, have what we desire. Another popular form of it is called *visualization*—holding a thought picture of what is desired in the consciousness for a sustained time until it manifests into our lives. This is based on the holistic law of "like attracts like," and is similar to the practices of native and shamanic medicine traditions. This was also the principle behind one of the central messages of Jesus when he said again and again, "Ask as if ye have already received."

That simple statement is loaded with layers of meaning and application that involve all levels of our being. The first obvious question is *"How* do we ask as if we have already received?" It seems that the "alchemical agent," or catalyst, between thinking a thing and actually having it, is *feeling*—we must change our feeling from one of lack to one of abundance.

And what would that feel like? It could be a feeling of excitement and anticipation, a feeling of relief that comes with release from worry or doubt, the peacefulness of knowing everything will be all right, the bliss of certainty, a feeling of connection and worthwhileness, and so on. Eventually, asking becomes not only a thinking and emotional art, but a psychosomatic one as our feelings, body chemistry, and internal energies change. This collaboration of thought/intent, emotion, and embodied feeling creates a vibrational empathy for abundance and possibility that cannot help but bring us what we desire, in one form or another.

In *The Isaiah Effect*, Gregg Braden refers to this as an actual technology—the "lost science of prayer" that has been restored to us through retranslation of the ancient Isaiah Scroll.

The Isaiah Scroll was discovered with the other Dead Sea Scrolls in 1946 and finally released for public study in the early

1990s. These scrolls contain sacred texts that ultimately became the Hebrew Torah and the Christian Old Testament; however, in many cases passages were "simplified" or omitted by fourth-century biblical compositors, camouflaging the deeper meanings of the original material. In the original Aramaic of this Scroll, we are told how to ask, revealing the thought/feeling/body "mechanics" that bring about an answered prayer: "All things that you ask straightly, directly . . . from inside my name, you will be given. . . . Ask without hidden motive and be surrounded by your answer. Be enveloped by what you desire, that your gladness be full" (*The Isaiah Effect*, p. 170).

As illustrated by Braden's story of a Native American friend who helped to end a local drought, this kind of asking is the difference between praying *for* rain and simply "praying rain." Here we change the feeling, or vibrations, of our past-present *internal* environment into feelings/vibrations that reflect a new condition as if it were already in place.

It is also important to note that Braden's friend started "praying rain" by expressing gratitude for the past condition of dryness. The teaching this gives us is that *all* things, people, and conditions come to serve us, albeit in ways that we may not understand until much later. Gratitude, which is vitally linked to acceptance and forgiveness, clears and cleanses our inner vibrational environment. By releasing ourselves from the weight of regret, remorse, guilt, or anger over past conditions, we make room to receive a new "future-present" that contains the things we desire.

This paradox of asking/becoming as if we've already received goes hand in hand with understanding that the Angels and the Divine "Stuff" they embody *already* exist within us. So although we may speak of asking for or inviting their presence, what we're really doing is inviting them to "quicken" inside the field of our own awareness. Thus asking becomes the catalyst that focuses our awareness, so that we can take the first step from lack and limitation to fullness and abundance.

2. Imbibing—Breathing in the Energetic "Elixir" of an Angel

This involves the *receiving* part of the asking process. If being willing to ask expresses choice, the willingness to receive expresses commitment. According to the Kabbalah (from the Hebrew "QBL" meaning "to receive"), it is the Divine's nature to emanate, pour forth, and give abundantly of Its fruits; it is mankind's challenge, opportunity, and sacred task to receive these gifts. Similar to the Christian concept of communion, the 72 Angels, and particularly our own Birth Angels, enable us to not only access and commune with, but actually *ingest* the Divine in order to magnify our own substance. This idea or symbolism of "eating God" has existed for eons in various traditions and tribal cultures, and it's usually accompanied by the belief that in so doing, one takes in and incorporates the attributes of the deity. To receive, or imbibe the 72 Angels of the Tree of Life, we must be *present* and *willing* to receive them. We already have all we would ask for within us, just as we already have within us all the qualities of the 72 Angels. Asking wakes up and focuses our awareness. Receiving puts that awareness into *interaction* by allowing the Angelic Energies to work their miracles within us.

To receive/imbibe an Angel, breathe in the "elixir" of its essence and meditate upon its energy. As the Isaiah Scroll says, "Be enveloped by what you desire." Allow feelings and ideas to come without judging or trying to change them. Trust that what you receive is what you truly need in your present circumstances. Let the vibration of sound silence your mental busy-ness and settle down into your heart until you feel the particular quality of Love it embodies. There's no need to pull or grasp or hold on to the Angels—allow them to hold you. In the presence of the Angels, simply be present so that you might receive the *present* that the Angel wants to give you of itself.

As indicated above, another form of asking as if you have already received is visualization. Rather than focusing on what you think you are not yet able to be, do, or have, focus your mind's eye on the fullest picture you hold in your heart of yourself and your life. Choose an Angel whose qualities reflect that picture. Visualize the Angel's energies entering and mingling with you. Allow the feeling of this Angelic commingling to permeate you. Have faith in the power of love embodied as that particular Angel to manifest in a way that is most relevant and true to who and where you are in that particular moment. Try not to control the means by which your vision will be realized. The art of receiving involves learning how to work with whatever shows up even if it happens to be different from what you desired or anticipated. Remember that whether or not you feel an immediate shift or effect, the truth and power of your heightened awareness has put into motion—even at the cellular level of your being—the intent that will ultimately manifest your vision.

3. Embodiment—Inner Shapeshifting

Beingness is the utmost result of asking and receiving. When you have become saturated and suffused with an Angel's essence, your base "mettle" is transformed into a finer substance as you come to **embody** the Angel and its qualities. It is at this stage that you remember your Divine identity by lending your physicality to the Divine Essence that dwells within you. You are at one with It, and It with you. There is no distance, discrepancy, or degree of separation between you and It. You have essentially come to manifest a part of the Divine that a particular Angel and its qualities represent. This is what every mystical tradition and practitioner aspires to attain—the ultimate union of physical, emotional, mental, and spiritual whole-beingness.

5.

FRUITS FOR
OUR LABORS

Eating from the Angelic Tree of Life Every Day

Most of us have busy, multidimensional lives no matter what our age or circumstances. From our teens and early adulthood, we begin building careers and financial resources, furthering our education, looking for love and eventually life partners, raising families, meeting challenges and opportunities, weathering change and adversities in health or life circumstances, and continuing to forge futures for ourselves, our dreams, and our offspring. Is there anything on this list that we could not use some extra help with?

No matter how busy we are, invoking the Angels, even by just speaking their names, will get their "Angel magic" working in every area of our lives. We can put the three-step process of working with the Angels in play daily by invoking them in the morning, imbibing them throughout the day, and practicing embodying their qualities as the day progresses. The last step, of course, will usually take longer than one moment's or day's effort, but behaving *as if* sets the stage and creates the inviting, affirmative attitude of acting as if we've already received.

There are as many ins and outs of accessing, communing, and comingling with the Angels as there are people and Angels. The following are some general guidelines:

1. *Work with the specific Angelic Energies governing the current five-day period, one-day period, and any 20-minute period* in the 24-hour day that corresponds to a significant event, encounter, or conversation.

2. *Work with your three (or four) Birth Angels and supporting Go and Return Angels* by focusing on the Angelic Virtues (and any Inversions that may show up) that correspond to your own particular purposes, challenges, and potentials. Since your Birth Angels will have the greatest ongoing relevance and potency with you, you may want to work with all three of them every day during their 20-minute periods of Intellect dominion.

3. *Work with the Angels closest to the date and time of your Birth Angels.* For example, if your Incarnation Angel is ROCHEL for March 1–5, and your actual birthday is March 1, you might want to check HABUHIAH, which corresponds to February 25–29, for Angelic qualities and functions also relevant to you. For your one-day Heart Angel, you might want to check the day before and after your birthday. And especially for your 20-minute Intellect Angel, check the 20-minute time periods before and after your birth time because the recorded time is often off by a few minutes.

4. *Work with a specific Angelic Energy that corresponds to a current activity, issue, challenge, or event in your life.* For example, consider working with the Angelic Energy or Energies that correspond to the time period of a daily meditation or workout. This will provide an opportunity to develop an ongoing relationship with the Angels presiding at that time. The same goes for working with an Angel or Angels that correspond to a particu-

lar issue or challenge. Whenever something occurs that triggers you in those areas, invoke the Angelic Energies whose qualities and functions support clearing and healing of those same areas.

5. *Work with the Birth Angels and Go or Return Angels of significant people in your life.* Some of your Birth Angels will likely be shared and represent qualities that complement or trigger mutual dynamics, issues, and challenges. As discussed in chapter 8, looking at relationship dynamics through the eyes of the Angels can help us to take difficulties less personally and utilize them as opportunities for growth.

To interact with the Angels regularly, you might keep a copy of the 72 Angels Chart next to your bed, in the kitchen, office, or anywhere you spend considerable time. This will enable you to check in every so often with the Angel of the day or current 20-minute period to note corresponding coincidences, synchronicities, encounters, significant issues, events, or relationship encounters. I have found that keeping a daily journal or calendar of interesting occurrences or connections—what I call "Angelic signs, synchronicities, and wonders"—has helped to increase my consciousness of "Angel activity." I also like to carry with me the descriptions of my particular Birth Angels and their qualities/functions to help refresh my daily awareness and communion with them.

Here's how you might orchestrate a particularly attentive day with the Angels:

1. *When you wake up in the morning, write down whatever dreams you remember.* Review them for any messages or symbols that may correspond to current issues or particular Angels you have been working with or feel compelled to work with. Before you get out of bed, check the Angels in dominion for that time and day, and speak their names. Invite them into your day. Meditate with their energies to set the tone for your day. Follow any

thoughts or feelings that come to mind when asking for help or guidance from a specific Angel. Perhaps a particular Angel's energies will correspond to a challenge or event relevant to your agenda that day. In addition, connecting with your Birth Angels will help to center you and "awaken" your ever-present "Angel-allies" to help you in your daily activities.

2. As you progress into your day, *be attentive to conversations, issues, events, and personal or business conflicts, etc., as they may correspond to the current daily or 20-minute Angel or your Birth Angels.* Receive everything and everyone as help—teachers or teachings that have been sent your way. Consider obstacles as opportunities for changing your approach, route, or destination. Treat seeming failures or rejections as a chance to redefine your purpose and strengthen your foundation or rethink and approach it from another angle. Do not despair if a wall seems impenetrable or a road relentless. These may be signals to look at whether or not you really want what's on the other side of the wall or at the end of that road. If not, consider changing your goals to more truly reflect who you are. Meanwhile, continue to invoke the qualities of the Angels currently in dominion, as well as your own Birth Angels, to enhance and bolster your resources.

3. *Notice your thoughts, moods, and attitudes and in what ways and why you are affected by certain situations or people.* Explore ongoing difficulties with significant partners, friendships, business associates, family, etc., by examining the corelatedness of your Angels and theirs. This can help you to better understand how even difficult dynamics in your relationships can provide opportunities for mutual learning.

4. *Be aware of any coincidences and synchronicities.* Your willingness to be helped by the Angels will increase both the quantity and quality of coincidence in your daily life. Within "intuitive reason," be open to people who initiate contact with you—even if they might seem at first to have little relevance to you or your current context. Set a destination, but let the path unfold. Try

not to resist—and even enjoy as a potential adventure—being diverted or rerouted. The gifts of synchronicity often wait in the detours, derailments, and seemingly inconsequential alleyways of our lives. Entering into the "dance of chance" is what gives our life the magical feeling that we are part of a greater flow and that somehow we are known by and in step with the universal "choreographer" of that flow.

5. Before you retire for the night, *recap the Angels you worked with that day and meditate briefly. Give thanks to all those, visible and invisible, who influenced or guided the course of your day. Expressing gratitude is a way of receiving all that has happened and been given to us.* It also helps to focus our awareness on what we already have and are. This can further expand our riches because of the power of thought to attract like form. Check the 20-minute Intellect Angel for your bedtime. Release and relax through your breath. Then speak or chant the Angel's name to breathe in the energy of its essence. Listen. Let any thoughts or seeming messages drift gently through your mind.

6. *Program your dreamtime to work on any issues or challenges you would like to see resolved or healed in your life.* As stated, dreams are often vehicles for personal messages to come to us from our invisible helpers when our conscious boundaries are relaxed. Sometimes we can actually work out fears and potential problems during our dreamtime. For example, I went through a period of time when I was apprehensive about having a car accident. And indeed I had a couple of close calls. One night, I dreamed that I actually did have a car accident. I woke up shaken—but I suddenly knew that the fear behind this dream was caused by a feeling that my life was careening out of control in certain areas. Once I understood this, I addressed those areas of concern and eradicated my fears as well as any "need" to work them out in the context of an actual accident.

7. *Before you turn out the light, check the Angel for the upcoming day and speak its name in acknowledgment.* This helps with dreamtime activities.

Since the Angel of the day (which will be in its heart dominion) actually changes at midnight, the first hours of the new Angel are occurring during our normal sleeping and dreaming hours. Thus, we can invoke a particular guardianship to watch over us until we awake. This can also include asking for that Angel's help to enhance the effectiveness of our dream-messages.

If we can learn to live without resisting our lives and their unfolding events, everything that comes our way will be an opportunity for discovery, adventure, and surprising gifts. We will have space inside and out for the Angels to walk with us, and eventually *as us*, every step of the way. With the Angels beside us, and inside us, stumbling blocks will turn into stepping-stones. Our positive attitudes and choices must be renewed every day in every situation that arises. Thus, by renewing our relationship with the Angels every day, we bolster our forces and resources exponentially. In other words, the Angelic Energies and their effects in our lives become cumulatively stronger. In the meantime, accepting our present circumstances—and ourselves just as we are—will allow the Angels to work with us in ways best suited to our needs and abilities at every given moment.

The Acceptance Factor

Acceptance is the antidote to resistance and provides the perfect environment for collaboration with our Angel-partners. Acceptance is sometimes confused with passivity or an unwillingness to change or rise to a challenge. It is lack of acceptance, however, that keeps us from *allowing* change or being willing to meet new circumstances that come our way. Whatever our present situation, the Angels can help us to experience the change that will move us on to the next thing. By being where we are and going with the flow, shift happens—even effortlessly.

Self-acceptance is one of the hardest things for us to do. Ironically, self-acceptance can be particularly difficult if you are on a conscious growth path—especially if you experience scenarios repeating in your life that you thought you had worked through. Immediately you feel as if you're "backsliding" or stuck going around with the same old wheel again—and how could that be when you've done so much work in that area! Here is where self-acceptance becomes vitally important to continuing progress and well-being. Self-acceptance frees us from the judgment that distracts or prevents us from reapproaching similar scenarios with a fresh eye to catch something we might have missed or not been ready for before.

Sometimes self-acceptance means accepting our present inability to accept. This is the ultimate form of self-acceptance. The paradox is always that once we give ourselves permission to be where we are, it is much easier to move to where we want to be. Allowing ourselves to be where we are puts our emotional feet squarely under us to give the most leverage and ballast for our next step—or leap. Another kind of self-acceptance can prompt us to simply remove ourselves from a situation or person. I have experienced again and again that the lessons we are here to learn *will* find their classroom. It is our right, and a kindness we must occasionally choose for ourselves, to change the classroom if it becomes too uncomfortable or unloving. That can mean taking a break from a relationship, friendship, or situation where you seem to be continually at odds, cross purposes, going in circles, and getting nowhere individually or together. Your soul's desire to grow all your parts will likely put you in another situation that may be similar, but where the learning process is less stressful or frustrating and, simply, kinder.

You are, I am, we all are entitled to learn our lessons in gentler ways. The trick is not to let guilt bully us into thinking we must submit ourselves to continual pain. If we are ever going to be able to practice one of our most common spiritual maxims, "Do unto others as you would have them do unto you," we must be able to conceive of—and receive—the lovingkindness toward ourselves that teaches us what that means. Self-acceptance is the greatest kindness we can extend to ourselves, and it is the precursor to accepting and being kind to others.

If the Angels can represent anything to us at all, let it be this: a reminder to be kinder to ourselves, to let the lessons of life be as gentle as the feel of a feathery light brushing against a child's cheek. Let us ask them to help us receive lovingkindness, and when the road is too rough, let us be lifted up and carried ever so lightly aloft in the folds of their compassion. Let us feel "in the arms of the Angels" that *nothing* is so heavy, not even ourselves, when we give our own heart sufficient weight.

6.

THE MAGIC AND MECHANICS OF THE 72 ANGELS

HOW the 72 Angels can help to transform our daily lives and relationships, overcome our challenges, and fulfill our purposes and potentials

As soon as our awareness becomes awakened to the Angels, our lives begin to change. Although our routines and circumstances may initially be the same, our lives become different because our perspective changes. We start to see everything and everyone in a different light. We come to sense the threads of connection between ourselves and others and the world at large. We become aware of the cause and effect of our choices. We realize that we are not alone as we witness the orchestration that underpins seemingly insignificant encounters or events. Ultimately, we begin to feel that we are not just being watched over, but in many ways we are continually being sent messages from the Angels especially for us.

The Language of "Angel-speak"

We can accelerate, heighten, and deepen our daily collaboration with the 72 Angels if we understand the signs, symbols, and synchronicities they use to get our attention and communicate with us. Although the Angels' rapport with us will probably be in a context that speaks specifically to each of us, the Angels have common ways of communicating that are recognizable once we start paying attention. We may hear them as a tiny voice in the wilderness of our minds, an ache or intuition in our hearts, or as a booming interloper bringing havoc or surprise to our expectations and plans. They may deliver their messages to us via startling exchanges with small children and animals, as writing on literal or metaphorical walls, or timely words, calls, and appearances from friends or strangers. Uncanny coincidences and encounters may seem to happen with greater frequency and relevance. People and situations will come along to help with our purposes, plans, or particular issues. Sometimes the Angels will orchestrate subtle, even humorous, synchronicities just to let us know they're here watching over us and available for "assignments."

I still fondly remember one "Angel-speak moment" that occurred with a local Federal Express courier a few years ago. I was waiting for a contract with an overseas publisher to arrive so that I could sign it and have funds wired into my bank account before leaving on a month-long business trip. The day before my departure it still had not arrived, and I remember saying aloud something like, "Oh I need an angel in my corner today . . ." Later that afternoon there was a knock on the door, and a courier who was evidently new on my route stood there with my contract, a sunny smile—*and a name tag on his jacket that said "Angel"!* Talk about feeling heard and watched over!

The Angels also work with us through the stories and symbols in our dreams, when our conscious minds are relaxed and more pene-trable. When I started interacting with the 72 Angels, I began to have dreams that contained scenarios, symbols, or explanations for the "Angel activities" I was experiencing. As the dream-messages contin-ued, there seemed to be a corresponding increase of "messages" exchanged in conversation with others that related to the qualities of a specific Angelic Energy governing that day or time period. When my friend Carolyn was pregnant with her first child, she awoke from a very clear dream one morning knowing that she must name her daughter Grace. It turned out that Grace was well named. She was so full of grace and contentment that she was affectionately called "Buddha-baby" by her family. Several years later, when Carolyn and I were introduced to the 72 Angels tradition, we discovered that one of Grace's Birth Angels is ALADIAH, corresponding to "Divine Grace."

With all the research, thinking, and writing that I have done about the 72 Angels tradition, most of my actual "contact" with the Angelic Energies comes with simplicity and lightness in every-day situations. A wonderful example of "out of the mouths of babes" came from Carolyn's second child, five-year-old Thomas, who is always spouting little wisdoms. He was bouncing on his bed one day and suddenly blurted out to his mother, "I have a lot of power, Mommy." Carolyn laughed and said, "Oh yeah, what is your power, Thomas?" Thomas banged his fist against his chest and yelled, "Love, love is my power!" One of Thomas's Birth Angels turns out to be JELIEL, for "Love and Wisdom."

How easily moments can turn into little messages and miracles when we are attentive and willing to allow the emissaries of love—whether of earthly or "heavenly" substance—to engage with us. The ongoing miracle is that all the while the Angels are working/play-ing/engaging with us, their qualities are mingling with and enlivening our own. Eventually, we are transformed, changed—reshaped from the inside out, to be the person we always dreamed we could be—our own true selves.

Angelic Virtues and Inversions

The 72 Angels tradition has a potentially liberating view of evil that corresponds uncannily to the fact that *in English evil spells "live"* *backward.* This could suggest that good and evil might be understood as a *going toward* or a *going away from* that which offers us light, love, and fulfullment.

Each Angelic Energy embodies the positive, creative, life-affirming qualities regarded as **Virtues** of the Divine, and each has a corresponding shadow, or dark, manifestation that results from unused or ill-used Virtues. The negative Angelic potentials are called **Inversions**—meaning they are indications or symptoms of a *backward* use of the light-love-life-affirming Virtues. When we work with the 72 Angels, we aspire to manifest their Virtues within ourselves. The areas where we struggle may show up as Inversions of those Virtues. However, in the eyes of the Angels, manifested Inversions are *symptoms* of a disturbance and therefore an *opportunity* for correction, realignment, and at-onement with ourselves and the Divine through the raising of our consciousness. Turning stumbling blocks into stepping-stones and disappointments into new determination is the best way to work with any inverted manifestations. Our Angelic allies are lovingly "programmed" to help us correct and realign without engaging in paralyzing self-judgment or guilt.

Angelic "Partners in Grime"

It is important to remember that the Angels work within our own choices. Ultimately, no matter how long we feel we've been "in the dark," we can change our context at any moment when we are finished with whatever we needed to learn by being there.

Thus, the Angels work with and within us as forces of love and healing to clear energetic clutter and give us more room for them and the bounty they bring. As they begin to dislodge the heaviness that anchors us to the past—unresolved issues, old fermenting wounds, harbored resentments, and angers—our lives can take on an accelerated quality that is sometimes magical and exhilarating, but at other times confusing or even painful. We may experience bouts of increased energy and joy, as well as periods of feeling sick or depressed as long-stored emotional and physical toxins start coming to the surface to be cleaned, healed, and released.

The degree of our acceptance or resistance to this "cleansing" will affect how much pain we experience and for how long. We should treat our "least" situations as soul-created opportunities for growth and change rather than as failures, mistakes, or punishment from life, God, or the universe. Regardless of how difficult or painful something is, consider that pain, of itself, is not meant to hurt but to indicate where we need healing. Therefore, *pain should be used as a pointer to the source problem.* If we follow this logic, we can eventually experience a healing of the source and a subsequent dissipation of the pain. If we become too uncomfortable during the process, help is always as close as our asking, receptive hearts. The Angels are specially equipped to handle whatever they may encounter within us. No emotional, physical, mental, or spiritual "grime" or swamp of difficulty within us is too thick for them to forge through or alleviate.

The Angelic Virtues and Inversions work together inside us the same way sand and the soft inside of the oyster do to shape the pearl. The work is deep and palpable—sometimes gritty and agitating, sometimes subtle and soft—but it ultimately yields something beautiful and valuable. As we continue to work with the 72 Angels, they become like a 72-pearled strand of Divine Wisdom that encircles our hearts and beautifies us from the inside. Finally, "Tikkun"—what the Kabbalah calls the process of fixing or correcting—is accomplished within us, and we accelerate along a course that will help to manifest the truest purpose and potential of our most wholly human self.

7.

OUR ANGEL-SELVES

our Birth Angels as inner "soulmates"

The quality of our relationships with others is directly impacted, even determined, by how we experience the relationship with ourselves. The healthier and more self-loving we are, the greater the well from which we may draw to love, respect, and care for others. Working with our Birth Angels helps us to know who we are and to become whole and "all-one" with ourselves. The Angels also give us a sense of the "other" that always lives within us. This ever-present other, our Divine counterpart which is composed in part of our Angelic "family," can cure the deep and secret loneliness so many of us feel and spend enormous amounts of time, energy and money trying to muffle or escape. Our Birth Angels are our invisible "soulmates"—our ultimate "match made in heaven"! As they mingle and merge with us, they show us what we are made of and what our true purposes are. As they bring us closer to the Divine within us, our human potential increases. Their ultimate goal is to glorify the Divine through the full emergence of our particular unique humanness.

I have seen uncanny matchups with so many people and their Birth Angels. The similarities usually show up as an Angelic correspondence to our own qualities, circumstances, interests, challenges, dreams, etc. An obvious correspondence is when a career choice directly reflects the qualities of one's Incarnation (life purpose) Angel. For example, Carolyn, my friend, has worked at least part of her career as a psychotherapist. Her Incarnation Angel is HABUHIAH, for "Healing," specifically on emotional and mental levels. Another friend, Jorgen, is a creative and intellectually rich person with deep spiritual interests who has also had much success in the pop songwriting world. His Incarnation Angel is HARAHEL, for "Intellectual Richness," whose qualities include a propensity for "remarkable practical/worldly intelligence with ability to manifest spirituality in worldly constructions . . . [including] the field of music."

My own Birth Angels still amaze me with their correspondence to my interests and issues: ARIEL, my Incarnation Angel, perfectly matches my endeavors in "perceiving and revealing . . . Divine mysteries and philosophical secrets" and LAUVIAH, my Heart Angel, for "victory [in love]," corresponds to the area of my greatest challenges. My Intellect Angels—JABAMIAH, the Angel of alchemy, represents a subject I've been interested in for years, and HAIYAEL, for Divine Warrior/Weaponry, corresponds to the meaning of my nickname, Terry, and the "warrior" posture I've had a tendency to favor in certain aspects of my life.[1]

It has been said that we are equipped with a means to deal with whatever afflictions or difficulties we are given. Some of those means include Angelic support. In one workshop I hosted for Christiane Muller, meditation teacher and guide in the 72 Angels

---

[1] As previously mentioned, we have two Intellectual Angels if our birth falls on a cusp time, i.e., on the hour or twenty minutes before or after.

tradition, two of the participants had multiple sclerosis, and both had Birth Angels whose Inversions included tendencies for an incurable disease. Both of these young women, however, were examples of people who saw their illness (Inversion) as an opportunity to cultivate the virtues of higher awareness, deeper self-discovery, and positive action—all of which was supported by the Virtues of their Birth Angels. Another woman whose childhood was traumatized by severely alcoholic parents had an Angelic Inversion of being a victim or sufferer of alcoholism. Her choice of profession as a therapist specializing in alcohol and substance abuse helped to turn that Inversion into a Virtue of understanding. This helped in her own healing and also gave her a deeper well from which she could minister to her clients. My chiropractor's son was born with a clef palate, which will require numerous surgeries throughout his young life. When I was preparing the infant's Birth Angels chart as a gift to his parents, I discovered that one of his Angels embodied qualities concerned with healing.

Another person I know, whose Incarnation Angel is POYEL, for "Fortune and Support," is often generous and supportive of others. Sometimes, however, he is paralyzed by extreme frugality, hoarding, and isolation, which are Inversions of POYEL. During these times he withdraws into himself and worries about money, despite the fact that he is financially very well-off. Working consciously with the Virtues of POYEL—as well as his Heart Angel, ANAUEL, which corresponds to "Perception of Unity"—can remind him that he is not alone and that connection with others can afford many opportunities for mutual abundance and support.

Another frequent Angelic match can show up in the role we play in others' lives. My friend Peg, whose Heart Angel is also POYEL, supported her son Tommy, who has cystic fibrosis, his whole young life with fierce love, determination, and faith. When Tommy was nine, Peg and her husband Tom helpd raise $25,000 for cystic fibrosis research. Nine years later, Tommy had become captain of his high school hockey team and was accepted to Notre

Dame, the school he always dreamed of attending. During that time, Peg and Tom, with the help of many friends and supporters, raised well over a million dollars for the continuing research that might one day enable their son and other children with cystic fibrosis to live out their dreams.

My friend Jodi, an actress, discovered her Birth Angels during important life shifts that involved career, friends, and family issues, the trauma of 9/11, and a much-needed time of healing. She gave me permission to tell some of her story as it relates to her new relationship with the Angels. Jodi came into my life through my compassionate niece Hannah, who asked me during the first anniversary week of 9/11 if she could bring Jodi up from the city to visit. Jodi had been near the World Trade Center that tragic morning and found herself, like so many others, running for her life. Having long suffered a fear of death, Jodi was traumatized that morning, but never sought counseling in the year after. It wasn't until the first anniversary of 9/11 that everything came crashing in for her. She had been experiencing that whole year the psychological trauma that tragedy can often compound upon a person who also has other unhealed issues.

Jodi stayed with us in the country for a few weeks. In fact, Hannah brought her up on what I later realized was her own (Hannah's) Incarnation Angel day—MELAHEL, for "Healing Capacity." We fed her some good food, took her for walks in the woods, and let her cry and talk. Eventually she began to heal. When she was stronger, she asked to help with an art project I was working on. As we worked, we started talking about the Angels, spirituality, and healing. She poked around my bookshelves and spent a lot of time reading and exploring different spiritual avenues. One day she got a call for an acting job to deliver a parable as Mother Teresa during an ecumenical gathering in New York City. Many of the world's most important religious leaders were there. This event impacted upon her the importance of healing intolerance and the idea of using her acting career in the service of more noble purposes. Jodi's Incarnation Angel is HAHAHEL, corresponding to "Mission" and the true meaning of the Christic principles that embrace people of all races, religions, and cultures.

Jodi is an example of how much a person's life can accelerate toward change when the Angels become activated in our consciousness. In the few months after she became aware of her Birth Angels, her life went through tremendous upheaval from negative to positive influences and outcomes. Jody was supported by her Birth Angels during difficult family encounters, and she is now learning new responses to old self-diminishing patterns. It's as if she is being totally rewired in her thought and feeling processes in ways that are perfectly calibrated to her personality, capacity, and circumstances.

Working with our Birth Angels as extensions of our own corresponding parts helps our different parts to work in tandem toward our wholeness. Even though there may be a particular area in which we have difficulty applying certain skills and attitudes, there is usually another area within us where the same skills and attitudes are working well. We can create miraculous change in our lives if we collaborate with the Angels to rehabilitate our "weaker" parts. Jody had the most difficulty understanding the implication of her Heart Angel, NEMAMIAH, for "Discernment." This corresponds to her difficulty understanding relationship dynamics—which also happens to be how the Inversions of NEMAMIAH manifest in her. Jodi's Intellect Angel, POYEL, is perfectly matched to her rational and analytical thinking processes and has helped provide ballast in the sea of her sometimes runaway emotions. Since the Virtues of POYEL through her intellect seem to be so focused and clear, I suggested that she call on POYEL to help transform the "acting out" Inversions of NEMAMIAH into Virtues. Furthermore, since POYEL and NEMAMIAH are right next to each other in their numerical order, their energies would naturally be complementary and mutually supportive.

I am learning to work with my Birth Angels in a similar way. My Heart Angel LAUVIAH's quality of "Victory" is positioned to work on the plane of my emotions in the contexts of love and wisdom. LAUVIAH's energies have helped me realize that for all the truths I might perceive and reveal, all the battles of existence I may fight and win, and all the transformation I might seek—without love driving my purposes I will not gain the true prize. I have come to see that the true prize, the "secret" that the Angels are here to reveal within us, is simply this: Love is everywhere, and it never leaves us. It may change its form, its face, or its voice from time to time—even from one minute to the next. But only when we stop resisting its changing forms will we see how its essence remains. In its Heart dominion, LAUVIAH's quality of "victory" becomes a victory of *perception through love,* which can dramatically affect how we experience relationships, aloneness, loss—and even victory itself.

Like the single stars that compose a constellation, each of our Birth Angels serves as a point of light helping us to form the pattern of our individual existences. Our Birth Angels come together within us to reflect a configuration of associations, influences, and connections that reveal the full scope of who we are and why we are here. Together, within us and through us, our Birth Angels reveal the greatest mystery of all—the Divine Itself at work and play within us.

8.

ANGELS AND RELATIONSHIPS

HOW the Angels help us to tap into the magic and meaning waiting in the wings of our relationships

You may notice as you begin to work with the Angels that you share Birth Angels and/or Go or Return Angels with important people in your life. The Virtues and Inversions of shared Angels often reflect the dynamics of relationships or encounters and reveal areas where greater understanding and growth is both needed and possible. In addition, new people may start showing up in your life whose Birth Angels correspond to yours and also to particular issues you may be dealing with at the time. This is a way the Angels externally introduce themselves in order for us to be more aware of and receptive to them internally.

Allowing the Angels to play a central role in our lives and our consciousness greatly enhances how we perceive and experience everything and everyone who crosses our path. Most of us know how wonderful it is to share special connections and correspondences with each other. Working consciously with our shared Angels can help to facilitate learning and growth in each other's lives not only at a heightened level of awareness, but also with a continually deepening, more meaningful experience of living, loving, and befriending.

A wonderful thing about working with the Angels is their tendency to ground our inner experience with an external confirmation. This goes along with their "job description" of bringing Heaven to Earth in their workings with us. From the first time I encountered the Angel POYEL ("Fortune and Support") in meditation, I felt a particular connection and sense of comfort and support. Soon people began to show up in my life who each had POYEL as one of their Birth Angels, and they all became integral supportive influences both personally and professionally. When I learned how to determine "Go" and "Return" Angels, I discovered that one of my own Birth Angel's corresponding Supporting Angels is POYEL. Experiencing POYEL through external encounters confirmed and supported my inner experience and helped ground POYEL within me even more profoundly.

So many people I know or have met briefly share Birth Angels with important friends, family members, partners, etc. The most common correspondence is a Heart Angel since there are five separate days that each Angel is in its heart dominion. For example, you and a friend might have different birthdays, but perhaps both of those days are governed by the same Angel. When you share an Angel with the same dominion—meaning that you and another have the same Incarnation Angel, Heart Angel, or Intellect Angel—your connection and influence with each other in that mutual area is likely to be very apparent. For example, my friend Lynn, who often has difficulties with love, has as her Heart Angel NEMAMIAH, for "Discernment." Lynn has always sought advice in discerning relationship issues from her older sister, Chris, who has fared well in matters of the heart. It turns out that Lynn and Chris both have NEMAMIAH as a Heart Angel. Lynn is an example of someone struggling with the Inversions of an Angelic Energy, while Chris is an example of someone manifesting the positive Virtues of that same Angel. The two sisters are close, and in fact Chris has long been a confidante and mentor to Lynn. All along, Chris has unknowingly helped Lynn to strengthen the positive qualities of their shared Angel.

During the months I was revising this book, I opened a small gallery in my hometown featuring original framed writings for gift-giving occasions. The gallery not only gives me a pleasant place to write without long hours of isolation, but it also has become a wonderful venue for magical and moving encounters. One day two women walked in, and I instantly noticed a strong bond and close warmth between them. They were drawn to the "Angel corner" in my store, and I overheard them reminiscing together. We began to talk, and I learned they had been best friends since childhood, had married in the same year, and sadly, both lost their husbands within a year of each other. They had, however, been a tremendous mutual solace for each other and had become even closer. A check of their birthdays revealed they had the same Heart Angel!

Three days before I delivered the first manuscript of this book to my editor, I was in my gallery writing and happened to look up. I saw a woman run by, then back up and come through the door. I felt her warmth and enthusiasm instantly. She told me she had been in New York City on business and had a compelling urge to get in her car and drive north. This "coincidental" meeting that came about through her willingness and trust was magical for both of us. Vanessa and I soon discovered we had some uncanny similarities, and we decided to go to dinner together. Eventually the subject of Angels came up, and we discovered that she and I have the same Heart Angel, LAUVIAH. We shared almost identical relationship issues. I had resolved mine by that point, but Vanessa still had to face some important decisions about hers. There were several other synchronicities and correspondences—one of which helped me clarify a particular point in my book. We were like angels for each other that day, bringing mutual gifts of insight and understanding with perfect timeliness.

When people have the same Birth Angels but in different areas of dominion, the correspondences can be more complex. In this kind of Angelic connection, we serve as external mirrors and catalysts for each other to help heal our own internal divisions and difficulties. These correspondences are often abrasive, annoying, and frustrating. However, they are usually also our greatest opportunities for releasing old karma and stifling attitudes. For example, I share the Angel ARIEL, my Incarnation Angel, with my mother; however, ARIEL is her Heart Angel. ARIEL's function of perceiving and revealing is played out within my mother through her heart and emotions. She does not have my particular interest in work or purpose involving esoteric discovery and study, and at times she has been sensitive about her lack of higher education. Attempts to share my passion for knowledge and new discoveries with her were often perceived as my trying to be a "know-it-all." This made me feel unappreciated and misunderstood and kept us perpetually resentful and misunderstanding each other. Realizing that my mother and I share the same Birth Angel in different areas of dominion has helped me to better understand our dynamic together. Through our shared Birth Angel we have been given the help to cross the seemingly great divide of our attitudes and fears. By meeting each other from our hearts, we have become better able to accept our differences. I have become more accepting of her ways of being and learning, and she is better able to appreciate my motives and even contributes insights and encouragement to some of my endeavors. The experience with my mother has helped to show me that *no matter how much knowledge we acquire or how great our intellect, Truth without the Love that turns knowledge into wisdom will always fall short of its own true purpose—to unite and make us whole within ourselves and with each other.* This is the Angels' teaching and the pearl that waits at the heart of every relationship.

The family sharing of Angels taps into a phenomenon I've

noticed again and again between parents and children. Family is a perfect scenario for Shakespeare's view of "all the world [as] a stage" where we act out our roles with each other. If we can observe and utilize the Angels' qualities as clues to help us understand ourselves and each other, maybe we can begin to take everyone's foibles, including our own, less personally. In this light, we can help each other become our best selves. This may include the opportunity to enjoy vicariously, without resentment or jealousy, an unfulfilled potential of our own, or to have a fear or difficulty forced into the open for airing, acceptance, and healing. By working with our Birth Angels to better understand ourselves and each other, we are given opportunities to resolve issues, enhance our own well-being, and positively energize family relationships.

My friend Ann has an eight-year-old daughter named Mariah who is a very independent, bright, and highly motivated young lady. One day Ann called and happened to mention that her daughter was having a distracted, unmotivated day and did not know what to do with herself. Interestingly, Ann had called me during the 20-minute Intellect period of ARIEL, my Incarnation Angel for perceiving and revealing. When I mentioned it to her, she laughed and said, "OK, tell me what the Angel was in the 20-minute period right before this when Mariah and I were having a small meltdown!" It happened to be the Intellect dominion of SEHALIAH, for "Motivation." To press the coincidence even more, this turned out to be Mariah's Heart Angel! Ann laughingly noted that Mariah seemed to be playing with the Inversion qualities of her Angel the whole day. Later that night, Ann thought about the correspondence between Mariah's Heart Angel and her unmotivated day. Suddenly she saw her daughter on a more objective level. Whenever Mariah was creatively engaged in a project, she was highly motivated and joyful with a strong self-initiative that needed no prompting from anyone else. However, when she was asked to do any type of mechanical or methodical activities, she immediately grew bored, unmotivated, and restless. That particular day had been full of activities Mariah did not enjoy or have an affinity for. At that moment, Ann gained a whole new appreciation for her daughter's intrinsic nature. She realized how she might be more sensitive to creating a balance of activities that would give consideration to Mariah's innate abilities and interests. Ann further realized that her own Incarnation Angel, IMAMIAH, for "Expiation of Errors," was a perfect energy for helping her "correct" or adjust her thinking. She also discovered that she and her daughter shared an Intellect Angel, NANAEL, for "Spiritual Communication (also one of my "Return" Angels). Mariah's "spirit" had communicated to her mother what she needed for her own well-being. Ann was able to receive the message and think through the dynamics of the day until she better understood her daughter's basic needs.

When I work with the Angels on a continual basis, new people often appear in my life who bring up the subject of Angels without knowing my background or interests. It usually turns out that we either have shared Birth Angels, or the day or moment of our meeting corresponds to one of their or my Birth Angels, or the current day's Angel corresponds to an issue one of us is presently dealing with that the other unknowingly bears a timely message about. Suddenly a perfect stranger becomes like an extended family member as we share the wonders of connection and synchronicity.

Once I was passing through London on a business trip and made last-minute arrangements to see my friend Connor, whom I hadn't seen in a couple of years. He was late but suddenly rushed in very excited and told me about all the unusual Angel experiences he had been having for the past week. Every time he turned around there was a sign with the word Angel on it, or a book about Angels, or a figurine of an Angel. In fact, he was late because he had just met someone named Angel and had stopped to talk with him. He didn't know yet that I was working with the 72 Angels tradition. When I told him about it, he realized that his whole week of "Angel activity" had been a preparation for our meeting. We checked to see what his Angels were—and we saw that, although he had been late, the exact moment he arrived was actually right on time for the 20-minute period of his own Intellect Angel! As we continued to talk and catch up with each other about the happenings of our lives, we both shared timely insights about our respective circumstances and challenges—some of which, corresponded to the Inversions of our Birth Angels.

Another striking "Angel-happening" was with my Swedish friend Jennifer. The last time I visited her in Sweden, I was struck by how heartful she seemed on that day. She exuded heart in everything she said and did. Before I left, we looked up her Angels and discovered that it was one of her Heart Angel days. I returned to the United States, and we didn't have the opportunity to speak for almost a year. On the very day I resumed work on this project after brief hiatus, Jennifer suddenly appeared at the door of my third-floor home office. She had only been to my house—which was way out in the country—once before. Somehow she managed to find it again and thought she would come by and surprise me. Amazingly, that day was one of my Heart Angel days.

Sometimes it seems as if the Angels are choreographing these kinds of meetings even before we know the other person exists. A couple of years ago I was flying home from a South American business trip and I had the Birth Angels book-in-progress with me. I began to work with the Angel ANAUEL, for "Perception of Unity," one of the Angels whose five Incarnation Days of dominion were coming up that next week. My work was interjected by discussions with my business associate about my current "singlehood." That next week during ANAUEL's Incarnation dominion, I met a man whose Heart Angel was ANAUEL. We began a relationship that ultimately gave each of us the opportunity to deal with some unresolved areas in our lives—all of which were present in the Virtues and Inversions of our respective Birth Angels and our "Go" and "Return" Angels, one of which, POYEL, we also shared. The "Angel dynamics" between us ultimately helped us to change our relationship when it became apparent that friendship was a better route for us.

My "surrogate" parents' Birth Angels not only seem to match

them so well, but are also perfectly complementary and supportive of their mutual qualities and purposes. I met Ken and Harriet on a bench in Central Park over 20 years ago. They are among the most remarkable people I have known because of their enthusiasm for loving, learning, and living their lives with such special consideration for each other. Harriet is a supportive and gently intelligent soul. Her Birth Angels are CAHETEL for "Divine Blessings," REHAEL for "Filial Submission," and YEIAZEL for "Divine Consolation and Comfort." Harriet, whose maiden name was Reich/Rich, was indeed richly blessed with comfort and abundance during her early family life in what was then Breslau, Germany. Everything changed, however, during Hitler's occupation of Germany when Harriet's fiancé was "confiscated" one night as they walked in a park together. Courageously, she risked Nazi imprisonment to personally deliver a contrived U.S. diplomatic telegram to Gestapo headquarters in order to obtain her fiancé's release from a concentration camp. She ultimately succeeded, and they escaped to the United States where they married and started a new life. Harriet's Incarnation Angel, CAHETEL, for "Divine Blessings," helps to "nourish, liberate, and transform one's way of living." This is in keeping with her experience. After securing her fiancé's rescue she left behind family properties, possessions, and the life that she had enjoyed—for the great blessing of being alive and free. Eventually, as their lives changed and the marriage waned, she was yet again blessed to start over with Ken, who has been her loving soulmate now for over 40 years.

Harriet and her Birth Angels' energies are perfectly supportive and comforting for her more intellectually intense husband, who happens to have two Intellect Angels. Ken's Incarnation Angel is LAVIAH for "Revelation," and his Heart Angel is HAZIEL for "Divine Mercy." His two Intellect Angels are OMAEL for "Fertility and Multiplicity" and LECABEL for "Intellectual Talent." Ken has always been fiercely interested in learning and "revelating." His fertile intelligence is a bottomless well from which he always draws worthwhile insights to share with others. When Ken was a child, he realized that his mother was chronically depressed and totally unreceptive to his joy and wonder of life. Very early on, Ken made a remarkably independent decision. He created a sanctity of space around himself in which his exuberant joy of life could not be tempered or contaminated. One of the qualities of Ken's Birth Angel, LAVIAH, is to "liberate from sadness and conflicts of the spirit that can occur when torn between higher and lower energies."

Other than a few "mechanical failures" now and then, as Harriet calls them, Ken and Harriet are healthy, happy individuals. Very early in life, each of them, in their own remarkable ways, put limits on how much they would allow negative or destructive circumstances, people, or energies to encroach on their time, compassion, and goodwill. These limits did not exempt members of their own families. Through their continual self-loving choices, they overcame much adversity as individuals and blossomed into two strong, healthy, and loving people. They are in their eighties and nineties now and still vital and enthusiastically interested in each other and in everyone who comes into their lives. They are my inspiration and a beautiful example of how people with very different characteristics can coexist lovingly and respectfully by appreciating each other's differences and viewing them as complementary rather than competitive.

We are all unique and necessary components of the whole. It is as if we live in a "universe"—"uni"/one "verse"—made up of millions of human letters, crossed *t*'s, dotted *i*'s and syllabic couplings! If we view the 72 Angels as embodiments of ourselves—our own different qualities and potentials in different states and degrees of growth and manifestation—they can help us to see others in the same light.

9.

A PATH FOR THE SPIRITUAL "EVERYMAN"

The similarity of the 72 Angels tradition
to other spiritual traditions, and why the
72 Angels are unique and powerful
companions for any heart on any road

The 72 Angels tradition enriches several esoteric traditions that have become increasingly appealing to seekers and self-helpers in the last few years, particularly: **angelology, astrology, Kabbalah,** and the ancient scientific and spiritual art of transformation called **alchemy.** The tradition also speaks to the interests of certain mystical branches of **Christianity** that have strived since the Middle Ages to reconnect Jesus, his messages, and actions to his Judaic and probable Kabbalistic roots. Furthermore, it contains elements that are strikingly similar to Buddhism and the Tao,

Japanese Shinto, Islam/Sufism, Hinduism, Neoplatonism, and Native American spirituality.

Angelology

Popular angelology trends can be confusing with their mix of Angels and Archangels and discrepancies of names, qualities, and functions. As discussed in chapter 1, the 72 Angels tradition imbues angelology with personal and particular relevance because each of the 72 Angels has a specific name, quality, function, and periods of influence that correspond to individual birth dates and times and specific qualities, purposes, and potentials. The 72 Angels make the Divine more accessible and the mystical less mysterious. They enable us to not only commune but interact with the Divine in ways that are practical, so that we might achieve real, palpable change in our lives. One of the important distinctions of this tradition is that the 72 Angels are offered not only as guardians and helpers, but as a means to become more Divine ourselves. We are meant to actually ingest these "edible" Angelic fruits of the Tree of Life (see Appendix I)—thereby our own human substance may become transformed and elevated.

Astrology

The 72 Angels give a whole new dimension and applicability to astrology. Since they are said to have emanated through the 12 houses of the zodiac on the way to their Sephirotic vessels, each Angel contains the qualities of particular astrological associations, as well as influences from the astrological aspects of its corresponding Sephira. The important distinction between angelology and astrology is that the 72 Angels are *embodiments* of the Divine *Person*, while the planetary bodies are *created objects* of the Divine. Therefore, the 72 Angels enable us, as multifaceted Human Persons, to engage directly with the multifaceted Divine Person. In the *Sefer Yetzirah* ("Book of Creation"), God directed Abraham not to rely too much upon astrological predictions. Likewise, we have often been cautioned against living our lives bound by astrological influences because our free will can override limitations that these influences might impose upon us. *Conversely, the 72 Angels tradition says that entering into a personal, conscious relationship with the Angels enables us to extend the reach of our free will.* The Angels do this by activating within us the Divine Attributes that they embody. This helps to clear us of energetic "static" or blocks that can prohibit the fulfillment of our potentials.

κabbalah

The Kabbalah is a vast and complex system that sees the Divine in all things and offers direct knowledge, experience, and recognition of the Divine Person and Principles within our own humanity. This tradition, preserved orally and in restricted texts for many centuries, is precise and yet mysterious, involving mathematics and mysticism, information and transformation, the mundane and the miraculous. Despite the Kabbalah's current popularity, its complexity and lack of any one definitive text can make it difficult to grasp. Many rabbis and Kabbalists, among them Rabbi David Cooper in his audio course, *The Mystical Kabbalah*, readily acknowledge the difficulty of accessing Kabbalistic mysteries for everyday use. The 72 Angels tradition, however, provides a practical way to interact with these sacred mysteries.

One of the core premises of the Kabbalah, which means "the receiving," is that the desire of the Divine to give is triggered by the desire of Creation to receive. The 72 Angels have been given to us to help focus our "requests" and elevate all our interactions. For every moment, issue, or challenge in our day there is a specific governing Angelic Energy that we may invoke. When we receive their energies, we activate the presence of the Divine within us. We tap into an eternal well of love and abundance "from which we might never go thirsty" and heighten our capacity to feel, think, and act more lovingly and purposefully in our very human lives.

Alchemy

Alchemy is about change—the total transformation of a person, substance, or system. Its principles are at the core of all mystical traditions, particularly the Kabbalah and the 72 Angels tradition. We can also see alchemy at play in the Christian concept of "grace," the mystical Hindu "Shaktipat," which awakens the Kundalini Fire of enlightenment, and the scientific concept of transmutation. The alchemical art and science of transformation reportedly originated with Hermes Trismegistus in Ancient Egypt and was later appropriated and developed as "Hermetics" by the Greeks. It was revived by Kabbalists, Neoplatonists, Gnostics, and other mystics and scholars throughout the Middle Ages and Renaissance, until the Spanish Inquisition drove it and other "magical" arts underground. Historically, scientific alchemy was concerned with the transmutation of substances, i.e., turning base metal into gold. Success was dependent upon the practitioner's corresponding spiritual ability to transform the base *mettle* of his or her own human substance into "golden" thoughts and deeds.

The Tree of Life is a symbol for "that which is above is like to that which is below." This is one of the core spiritual premises of alchemy as found in the "Emerald Tablet" writings, attributed to Hermes. This statement is the foundation for the Judeo-Christian concept that Heaven/Divine (macrocosm) is a template for Earth/humankind (microcosm). It is in the context of this "as above, so below" relationship between Heaven and Earth that we are made in the "image and likeness" of the Divine and that all we think, feel, or do reverberates back to and affects the Divine. This mutual cause and effect dynamic between Heaven and Earth is symbolized by the Tree of Life. The 72 Angels are the fruits that disseminate the seeds of the Tree, which help to root the transformative principles of the Divine in the earthly soil of Humanity.

The Angels and Modern Alchemy

The modern descendant of scientific alchemy is chemistry. Interestingly, the metaphor of alchemy, and the actual word itself, has been further revived and reappropriated in our second millennium world in numerous other fields. A quick perusal of one of the major online bookstores turned up no less than 692 current publications with the word "alchemy" in their titles. They deal with the fields of psychology and self-help, health and medicine, philosophy, music, physics, politics, business and banking, advertising, cosmetics, etc. Perhaps the underlying message of this revived interest in alchemy might be that our motives and machinations in general, and particularly our relationships with ourselves and each other, require transformation if we intend to maintain a viable planet. On a social level, the result of alchemical transformation would not only be politically correct—or "tolerant" behavior among differing peoples and nations—but would enable us to actually honor, embrace, and enjoy each other's differences as parts of a whole we all belong to. These fundamental changes in perspective, which can create lasting behaviorial changes, are the work of the Divine and the Angelic emissaries of love. And these are the things that the Angels can accomplish within us.

other traditions

The 72 Angels tradition contains identical elements to some of the core messages of all traditions. It can appeal to those who desire to enliven their own religious practice, as well as to individuals seeking a more autonomous route to the Divine. The practical work with the 72 Angels that involves asking and receiving echoes the Christian theme of "ask and ye shall receive." Christian Kabbalists of the Middle Ages regarded Jesus as a fulfillment of Kabbalistic mysteries. They saw him as a man who became "Christed"—a man who was so totally receptive to the Divine and so filled with Divine qualities that he actually came to embody the Divine and Its message of Love. The 72 Angels may be thought of as 72 "refractions," tones, colors, expressions, and qualities of that Divine Love. They might also be compared to the seeming pantheon of the Hindu, Native American, and other traditions that worship various qualities or facets of the "Brahman" or "Great Spirit" as different names, faces, and forms of the One Divine Energy or Being known in the Western world as God. The Kabbalistic Tree of Life is very similar in its form and function to the Sufi (mystical branch of Islam) Tree of Life. The Sephirot in which the 72 Angels "reside" on the Tree of Life also correlate to the Vedic energy spheres known as chakras in the human body. Caroline Myss's *Anatomy of the Spirit* presents a fascinating comparison of the seven lower Sephirot of the Kabbalistic Tree of Life, the seven Christian sacraments, and the seven Vedic chakras. Thai mysticism speaks about how the spirit inside which they call "khwan" resides in the different body parts as "32 mini-khwan." *Soul Retrieval*, by Sandra Ingerman, suggests the 32 branches, or paths, of the Tree of Life. The Buddhist tradition encourages its practitioners to aspire to Buddhahood by purification and transformation of mind, heart, and body. Similarly, the alchemical dynamic of the 72 Angels can burn off the sludge of debilitating emotions and thoughts that leaden, and ultimately deaden, our existence—until our inner and outer environments are purified and transmuted into what the Tao calls "the golden mean" of being, or what Japanese Shinto calls "walking the way of the kami" (gods).

How the 72 Angels fit into our world Today

The 72 Angels remind us that "God" is made up of many qualities, and that those qualities—which are embodied as the Angels, human beings, and every other created thing—are also made of God. Like the cliché "the apple doesn't fall far from the tree," each thing and being created by the Divine—however small or great—embodies particular aspects of the image and likeness of That Which created it.

Therefore, each human life represents a fragment of the Divine's total identity and being, and it takes every one of us and all of us to complete the "Bigger Picture." And like a giant jigsaw puzzle, each piece of Creation is imprinted and shaped with a unique portion of the picture. If a piece is missing or in the "wrong" place, the picture is distorted or incomplete, and thus not whole. Though we sometimes struggle with recognizing—and remembering—which piece we are and where our place is, having the Bigger Picture as a blueprint can help us to find where we belong both in the overall picture and in the picture of our individual lives.

The 72 Angels are the conveyors of this blueprint and the cosmic reflection that there is a unique and important place for every single one of us. They remind us that as an embodied quality of God, each one of us has means within to reconnect to our Source that was and continues to be given to us by the Source Itself. As evidenced by the many gurus, prophets, saints, mystics, teachers, and practitioners of our various traditions throughout time, it could be justifiably argued that whatever path a seeker chooses, the Divine will meet and accompany that individual on his or her journey in a manner and language that most speaks to the ways and purposes of that individual and the culture within which he or she lives. For the sake of love and global harmony, it is worth considering that *the depth and authenticity which so many individuals or groups experience with their particular religious/spiritual affiliations is a testimony not to any "only Truth," but to the nature of the Divine to be everything and everywhere.* In other words, the Divine so loves and respects us that It is willing to meet us wherever and whoever we are.

The discovery and revival of this heart-driven Renaissance tradition of the 72 Angels is very timely. Whether a seeker desires to walk a private path to the Divine, or to rejuvenate an organized spiritual practice, the 72 Angels can be facilitators. This is because their venue is the human heart—something all of us have in common, whatever language we speak or ideologies we express. The love that the Angels bring is like a 72-colored rainbow radiating the infinite combinations of Divine hues that we as humans embody and express. This is a love that contains all true purposes and possibilities. It is a love with as many different qualities, forms, faces, and expressions as there are people. It is a love that waits on us to discover that however long or far we seek, what we are looking for is always right here, in our heart of hearts, prompting us to ask, beckoning us to receive, inviting us within—to be with it—and to know once and for all that, truly, we are never alone.

APPENDIX I

ORIGIN AND PURPOSE OF THE TREE OF LIFE

In the 72 Angels tradition, everything from the beginning of Creation has its root in the symbolic Tree of Life, and has been endowed with Divine Essence. The sacred principles kept alive by the Tree of Life continually fertilize not only the power of the spoken word, but also the energetic significance of the names and descriptions we attribute to things and people. This is the cosmology that supports the idea in many schools of thought that the things we think and speak inevitably become manifested forms in reality.

The Tree of Life is commonly known as one of the two sacred trees in the biblical account of Creation and the Garden of Eden. Adam and Eve were allowed to eat from the Tree of Life until they disobeyed God and ate from the Tree of Knowledge of Good and Evil. As punishment for their "original sin" of disobedience, they were expelled from the Garden and also forbidden to partake of the Tree of Life and its eternal fruits.

In the literal biblical stories, God's punishments or threats of punishment were sometimes later modified or retracted altogether. According to Genesis, the first book of the Old Testament, the initial populating of Earth was followed by further human disobediences and transgressions. Then God punished mankind with the Great Flood, which destroyed all creatures except Noah, his family, and the creatures aboard the Ark. Then came a subsequent repopulating of Earth with God's promise that, despite mankind's continuing fallibility, we would not be punished by flood again. The later story of Jonah and the whale and the saving of the city of Nineveh recounts another Divine reprieve when Nineveh heeds the warning Jonah so reluctantly, but finally, delivered to the city.

Christianity is based upon the New Testament/Covenant, which is yet another new or "updated" promise. It could also be viewed as a map for the way back to the Garden. Here, God's new Word, or "Logos," is embodied by Jesus the Christ. Jesus' message acknowledged that despite mankind's continuing fallibility, we might return to the heart of God and be "saved" through the graces of love, forgiveness, and faith. *By allowing these graces to take root within us, we may, within our human essence, be restored to the Garden, the Tree of Life, and the presence of the Divine.*

This idea of return, so often echoed in our emotional and spiritual longings for "home," plays to another important concept in the Kabbalistic view of the Tree of Life. Not only are we humans the effect of Divine Cause, but we also cause an effect on the Divine and its cosmic hierarchies by our thoughts, feelings, and actions on this earthly plane.

> When we seek to balance the imbalances of our world, we heal our world. And when we heal imbalances on the micro level, it causes a ripple effect up the Tree to heal the upper worlds as well. . . . What occurs in the upper sefirot [worlds] reflects what occurs in the lower sefirot [worlds], but what occurs in the lower . . . also stimulates change in

the upper . . . , so that the next round of energy that flows down to us is altered.—Kim Zetter, *Simple Kabbalah*

It matters what we do here, for we continually affect and *effect* so much more than we can ever know. In this respect, the Tree of Life reminds us that each of us have our own place or home within the Tree, and everything we think and do is felt and known on some level or another not only by the Tree's inhabitants, but also by the Tree itself.

The Tree of Life's 32 Branches

The Tree of Life is a symbolic "flow chart" for the descent of the Unknowable Divine Mind into knowable Human Beingness. The Divine Oneness differentiated Itself via the expulsion of sound into 10 spheres, or vessels, of energy called the Ten Sephirot—which then manifested further diverse forms of creation. The Tree's 32 branches, or "Paths" of Wisdom, are composed of these Ten Sephirot and the 22 Creator-sounds (letters of the Hebrew alphabet) that connect them.

The number 32 relates metaphorically to Universal Man ("Adam Kadmon") and our 32 teeth, including wisdom teeth, for chewing and ingesting life in all its aspects in order to extract the nutrients and achieve wisdom. The Tree as a symbol for two-way communication between the Human and the Divine corresponds to the 32 nerve pathways in the human spinal-cranial network that conduct messages to and from the mind. The number 32 also corresponds to the numerical value of the Hebrew word for "heart." This applies to both the heart of the Tree of Life, where the Angels reside, and the human heart, where the Angels meet us to help reconnect us to our Divine origin. Ultimately, the number 32 represents the saturation of Divine consciousness within the human vehicle.

When we get to number 33, we "pass over" into the realm of unearthly mysteries and "initiatic knowledge." This corresponds to the thirty-third Path on the Tree, the invisible Sephira Da'ath, which signifies ascendance into the Divine mysteries, and is said to be unapproachable until all 32 branches of the Tree have been mastered. Likewise, 33 corresponds to the fulfillment of Jesus' earthly life and his ascendance to eternal life, which enabled the release of the Holy Spirit and the offering of Divine Mysteries to all mankind.

Like the manifested Christ, the Tree of Life might be viewed as a bridge between the Old and New Covenants—a spiritual vehicle by which we may return to "at-onement" with our Divine "Father" from the "prodigality" of "original sin." Therefore by reappropriating the Tree of Life on a metaphorical level, we can reclaim and reintegrate our spiritual nature into our physical, emotional, and intellectual natures. This was the purpose of the medieval multitraditioned Kabbalists, mystics, and scholars who came together to decipher and enliven ancient texts dealing with Creation and other Divine revelatory material. Thanks to their visionary work, we have the symbology of the Tree of Life and its "edible" Angelic Fruits as a very powerful means to partake of the Divine while in human form.

APPENDIX II

SOURCES USED

Agrippa, Henry Cornelius, *Three Books of Occult Philosophy*, Llewellyn Publications, 1993.

Aïvanhov, Omraam Mikhaël, *Angels and Other Mysteries of The Tree of Life*, Prosveta, 1994.

———, *The Fruits of the Tree of Life: The Cabbalistic Tradition*, Prosveta, 1991.

———, *The Zodiac, Key to Man and to the Universe*, Prosveta, 1989.

Berg, Dr. Philip S., *Kabbalah for the Layman, vol. 1*, The Press of the Research Center of Kabbalah, 1988.

Braden, Gregg, *The God Code*, Three Rivers Press, 2004.

———, Gregg, *The Isaiah Effect*, Three Rivers Press, 2000.

Cooper, David A., *God Is a Verb*, Riverhead Books, 1997.

Evola, Julius, *The Hermetic Tradition*, Inner Traditions International, 1995.

Fontana, David, *The Secret Language of Symbols*, Chronicle Books, 1993.

Freke, Timothy, and Peter Gandy, *The Hermetica: The Lost Wisdom of the Pharoahs*, Jeremy P. Tarcher/Putnam, 1999.

Godwin, David, *Cabalistic Encyclopedia*, Llewellyn Publications, 1999.

Godwin, Gail, *Heart: A Personal Journey Through Its Myths and Meanings,* William Morrow, 2001.

Godwin, Malcolm, *Angels: An Endangered Species,* Simon and Schuster, 1990.

Hall, Manly P., *Secret Teachings of All Ages,* The Philosophical Research Society, 1997.

Hanson, Kenneth, *Kabbalah: Three Thousand Years of Mystic Tradition,* Counsel Oak Books, 1998.

Hauck, Dennis William, *The Emerald Tablet,* Penguin/Arkana, 1999.

Haziel, Les Anges, *Le Grand Livre du Tarot Cabalistique,* Editions Bussière, 1991.

——, *Possibilités Capacités et Pouvoirs Conférés par les Anges,* Editions Bussière, 1989.

Hoffman, Edward, *The Hebrew Alphabet,* Chronicle Books, 1998.

Ingerman, Sandra, *Soul Retrieval: Mending the Fragmented Self,* HarperSanFrancisco, 1991.

Kaplan, Aryeh, *Sefer Ytezirah: The Book of Creation,* Samuel Weiser, 1997.

Matt, Daniel C., *The Essential Kabbalah,* HarperSanFrancisco, 1995.

Matt, Daniel Chanan, trans. *Zohar: The Book of Enlightenment,* Paulist Press, 1983.

Meera, Mother, *Answers,* Meeramma, 1991.

Mitchell, Stephen, *Tao Te Ching,* HarperPerennial, 1988.

Pagels, Elaine, *The Gnostic Gospels,* Vintage Books, 1989.

Parfitt, Will, *The New Living Qabalah: A Practical and Experimental Guide to Understanding the Tree of Life,* Element, 1995.

Prophet, Elizabeth Clare, *Kabbalah: Key to Your Inner Power,* Summit University Press, 1997.

Ramsay, Jay, *Alchemy,* Thorsons, 1997.

Teasdale, Wayne, *The Mystic Heart,* New World Library, 2001.

Zetter, Kim, *Simple Kabbalah,* Conari Press, 1999.

Zukav, Gary, *The Seat of the Soul,* Simon and Schuster, 1989.

QUICK REFERENCE CHARTS

The Tree of Life

The Tree of Life is a highly systematic symbol used by Kabbalists as a template for the creation of the universe and mankind's origin from likeness and relationship to the Divine (as Adam Kadmon, the universal man). According to the Kabbalah, the "Divine Unknowableness" (Ain→Ain Soph→Ain Soph Aur) differentiated its Oneness into 10 regions or Aspects of Itself, represented by the Ten Sephirot (singular Sephira). The Ten Sephirot and the 22 Paths that connect them comprise the 32 Paths of Divine Emanation that are sometimes called the 32 Paths of Wisdom. These relate metaphorically to the 32 teeth of a human being and the importance of chewing and ingesting life in all its aspects in order to extract the nutrients and achieve wisdom. Kabbalists say that the Divine (macrocosm) Tree of Life emanated a mirror image of itself into Creation (microcosm), having roots in Heaven that blossomed into Creation in order to establish roots of the Divine on Earth. It is a symbol for one of the central doctrines of the Kabbalah, attributed to the great alchemist Hermes Trismegistus as "that which is below is like to that which is above." This was similarly stated by Jesus as "Thy will be done on Earth as it is in Heaven," and more subtly by the Tao as "Only in being lived by the Tao can you be truly yourself." This "as above, so below" paradigm is key to understanding the cause and effect relationship between the Divine and Creation.

DA'ATH, sometimes referred to as the "invisible" or "dark" Sephira of the 33rd Path, represents the Infinite Knowledge that lies beyond the Abyss which may not be approached except by one who has first mastered and embodied the 32 Paths.

The Four Planes of Existence represent the order of Divine Emanations that resulted in creation of the Universe and the Kingdom of Earth. These four planes correlate to the spiritual, emotional, intellectual, and physical aspects of the Human Self. The World of Emanations (Sephirot 1–3) can be said to represent ideas formulating in the mind of God/Man; the World of Creation (Sephirot 4–6), the orchestrating and planning of those ideas; the World of Formation (Sephirot 7–9), the gathering of materials for implementation; and the World of Action (Sephira 10), as ideas/Universe/Creation manifested into being.

The 22 Paths that connect the Ten Sephirot correspond to the 22 letters of the Hebrew Alphabet. They represent the 22 Divine sounds of Self-expression that brought the universe into being.

The division of the Tree of Life into three vertical Pillars is a way of showing the necessity for the balance of extremes in Divine and human relationships. For each created thing and being in the universe to be in harmony, all opposing factors must be continually reconciled by coming toward each other to meet at the center.

THE TREE OF LIFE AND THE TEN SEPHIROT

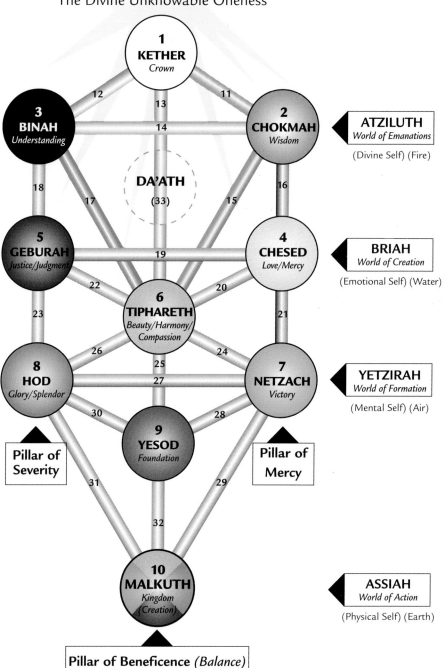

AIN
AIN SOPH
AIN SOPH AUR
The Divine Unknowable Oneness

1
KETHER
Crown

12 13 11

3
BINAH
Understanding

14

2
CHOKMAH
Wisdom

◀ **ATZILUTH**
World of Emanations
(Divine Self) (Fire)

18 17

DA'ATH
(33)

15 16

5
GEBURAH
Justice/Judgment

19

4
CHESED
Love/Mercy

◀ **BRIAH**
World of Creation
(Emotional Self) (Water)

22 20

23

6
TIPHARETH
*Beauty/Harmony/
Compassion*

21

8
HOD
Glory/Splendor

26 25 24

27

7
NETZACH
Victory

◀ **YETZIRAH**
World of Formation
(Mental Self) (Air)

30 28

**Pillar of
Severity**

9
YESOD
Foundation

**Pillar of
Mercy**

31 29

32

10
MALKUTH
*Kingdom
(Creation)*

◀ **ASSIAH**
World of Action
(Physical Self) (Earth)

Pillar of Beneficence *(Balance)*

THE 72 ANGELS OF THE TREE OF LIFE — DAYS and HOURS OF DOMINION

ASK (Invoke the Angels by Name) that you may RECEIVE (Eat of Their Fruits) and BE as They are (Embody Their Qualities)

The 72 Angels of the Tree of Life represent the 72 Names and Person of the Divine. These Angelic Energies emanated as differentiated aspects of the Divine at the beginning of Creation through the 360 degrees/12 signs of the zodiac into 9 of the Tree's Ten Sephirot;[1] thereby what was "Above" became manifested and embodied "Below." Each of us has the support and influence of at least three of these Angelic Aspects, which correspond to our date and time of birth and lifelong potentials, purposes, and challenges. Our Incarnation Angel (five-day period of birth) expresses Divine Will and corresponds to our physical birth and will to fulfill our life purpose. Our Heart Angel (actual day of birth) expresses Divine Love and corresponds to our emotional plane. Our Intellect Angel (20-minute period of birth) expresses Divine Mind and corresponds to our human intellect and ability to utilize Divine Principles in our lives. Those born at a "cusp" time (on the hour or exactly 20 minutes after or before), have two Angels for the mental plane.

---

[1] The Tenth Sephira, MALKUTH, corresponds to the Kingdom of Saints and Beatified Souls.

1 KETHER
Crown, Divine Will

Name of Angel—Primary Quality	Incarnation Angel — Physical Birth and Life Purpose (Five-Day Period of Birth)	Heart Angel — Qualities and Use of Emotions (Actual Birth Day)					Intellect Angel — Qualities and Use of Intellect (Birth Time)
1 VEHUIAH — Will and New Beginnings	3/21-25	3/21	6/3	8/17	10/30	1/9	12:00-12:20 A.M.
2 JELIEL — Love and Wisdom	3/26-30	3/22	6/4	8/18+19 A.M.	10/31	1/10	12:20-12:40 A.M.
3 SITAEL — Construction of Universe/Worlds	3/31-4/4	3/23	6/5	8/19 P.M. + 20	11/1	1/11	12:40-1:00 A.M.
4 ELEMIAH — Divine Power	4/5-9	3/24	6/6	8/21	11/2	1/12	1:00-1:20 A.M.
5 MAHASIAH — Rectification	4/10-14	3/25	6/7	8/22	11/3	1/13	1:20-1:40 A.M.
6 LELAHEL — Light (of Understanding)	4/15-20	3/26	6/8	8/23	11/4	1/14	1:40-2:00 A.M.
7 ACHAIAH — Patience	4/21-25	3/27	6/9	8/24	11/5	1/15	2:00-2:20 A.M.
8 CAHETEL — Divine Blessings	4/26-30	3/28	6/10	8/25	11/6	1/16	2:20-2:40 A.M.

2 CHOKMAH
Wisdom

Name of Angel—Primary Quality	Incarnation Angel Physical Birth and Life Purpose (Five-Day Period of Birth)	Heart Angel Qualities and Use of Emotions (Actual Birth Day)					Intellect Angel Qualities and Use of Intellect (Birth Time)
9 HAZIEL Divine Mercy and Forgiveness	5/1–5	3/29	6/11	8/26	11/7	1/17	2:40–3:00 A.M.
10 ALADIAH Divine Grace	5/6–10	3/30	6/12+13 A.M.	8/27	11/8	1/18	3:00–3:20 A.M.
11 LAUVIAH Victory	5/11–15	3/31	6/13 P.M.+14	8/28	11/9	1/19	3:20–3:40 A.M.
12 HAHAIAH Refuge, Shelter	5/16–20	4/1	6/15	8/29	11/10	1/20	3:40–4:00 A.M.
13 YEZALEL Fidelity, Loyalty, Allegiance	5/21–25	4/2	6/16	8/30	11/11	1/21	4:00–4:20 A.M.
14 MEBAHEL Truth, Liberty, Justice	5/26–31	4/3	6/17	8/31	11/12	1/22	4:20–4:40 A.M.
15 HARIEL Purification	6/1–5	4/4	6/18	9/1	11/13	1/23	4:40–5:00 A.M.
16 HAKAMIAH Loyalty	6/6–10	4/5	6/19	9/2	11/14	1/24	5:00–5:20 A.M.

Understanding

Name of Angel—Primary Quality	Incarnation Angel Physical Birth and Life Purpose (Five-Day Period of Birth)	Heart Angel Qualities and Use of Emotions (Actual Birth Day)					Intellect Angel Qualities and Use of Intellect (Birth Time)
17 LAVIAH Revelation	6/11–15	4/6	6/20	9/3	11/15	1/24	5:20–5:40 A.M.
18 CALIEL Justice	6/16–21	4/7	6/21	9/4	11/16	1/25	5:40–6:00 A.M.
19 LEUVIAH Expansive Intelligence/Fruition	6/22–26	4/8	6/22	9/5	11/17	1/26	6:00–6:20 A.M.
20 PAHALIAH Redemption	6/27–7/1	4/9	6/23	9/6	11/18	1/27	6:20–6:40 A.M.
21 NELCHAEL Ardent Desire to Learn	7/2–6	4/10	6/24	9/7	11/19	1/28	6:40–7:00 A.M.
22 YEIAYEL Fame, Renown	7/7–11	4/11	6/25	9/8	11/20	1/29	7:00–7:20 A.M.
23 MELAHEL Healing Capacity	7/12–16	4/12	6/26	9/9	11/21	1/30	7:20–7:40 A.M.
24 HAHEUIAH Protection	7/17–22	4/13	6/27	9/10	11/22	1/31	7:40–8:00 A.M.

4 CHESED
Love and Mercy

Name of Angel— Primary Quality	Incarnation Angel Physical Birth and Life Purpose (Five-Day Period of Birth)	Heart Angel Qualities and Use of Emotions (Actual Birth Day)					Intellect Angel Qualities and Use of Intellect (Birth Time)
25 NITH–HAIAH Spiritual Wisdom and Magic	7/23–27	4/14	6/28	9/11	11/23	2/1	8:00–8:20 A.M.
26 HAAIAH Political Science and Ambition	7/28–8/1	4/15	6/29	9/12	11/24	2/2	8:20–8:40 A.M.
27 YERATEL Propagation of the Light	8/2–6	4/16+17 A.M.	6/30	9/13	11/25	2/3	8:40–9:00 A.M.
28 SEHEIAH Longevity	8/7–12	4/17 P.M. + 18	7/1	9/14	11/26	2/4	9:00–9:20 A.M.
29 REIYEL Liberation	8/13–17	4/19	7/2	9/15	11/27	2/5	9:20–9:40 A.M.
30 OMAEL Fertility, Multiplicity	8/18–22	4/20	7/3	9/16	11/28	2/6	9:40–10:00 A.M.
31 LECABEL Intellectual Talent	8/23–8/28	4/21	7/4+5 A.M.	9/17	11/29	2/7	10:00–10:20 A.M.
32 VASARIAH Clemency, Equilibrium	8/29–9/2	4/22	7/5 P.M.+6	9/18	11/30	2/8	10:20–10:40 A.M.

5 GEBURAH
Justice, Judgment, Strength

Name of Angel—Primary Quality	Incarnation Angel Physical Birth and Life Purpose (Five-Day Period of Birth)			Heart Angel Qualities and Use of Emotions (Actual Birth Day)			Intellect Angel Qualities and Use of Intellect (Birth Time)
33 YEHUIAH Subordination to Higher Order	9/3–7	4/23	7/7	9/19	12/1	2/9	10:40–11:00 A.M.
34 LEHAHIAH Obedience	9/8–12	4/24	7/8	9/20+21 A.M.	12/2	2/10	11:00–11:20 A.M.
35 CHAVAKIAH Reconciliation	9/13–17	4/25	7/9	9/21 P.M.+22	12/3	2/11	11:20–11:40 A.M.
36 MENADEL Inner/Outer Work	9/18–23	4/26	7/10	9/23	12/4	2/12	11:40–Noon
37 ANIEL Breaking the Circle	9/24–28	4/27	7/11	9/24	12/5	2/13	Noon–12:20 P.M.
38 HAAMIAH Ritual and Ceremony	9/29–10/3	4/28	7/12	9/25	12/6	2/14	12:20–12:40 P.M.
39 REHAEL Filial Submission	10/4–8	4/29	7/13	9/26	12/7	2/15	12:40–1:00 P.M.
40 YEIAZEL Divine Consolation and Comfort	10/9–13	4/30	7/14	9/27	12/8	2/16	1:00–1:20 P.M.

6 TIPHARETH
Beauty, Compassion, Harmony

Name of Angel— Primary Quality	Incarnation Angel Physical Birth and Life Purpose (Five-Day Period of Birth)			Heart Angel Qualities and Use of Emotions (Actual Birth Day)			Intellect Angel Qualities and Use of Intellect (Birth Time)
41 HAHAHEL Mission	10/14-18	5/1	7/15	9/28	12/9	2/17	1:20–1:40 P.M.
42 MIKAEL Political Authority and Order	10/19-23	5/2	7/16	9/29	12/10	2/18	1:40–2:00 P.M.
43 VEULIAH Prosperity	10/24-28	5/3	7/17	9/30	12/11	2/19	2:00–2:20 P.M.
44 YELAHIAH Karmic Warrior	10/29-11/2	5/4	7/18	10/1	12/12	2/20	2:20–2:40 P.M.
45 SEHALIAH Motivation, Willfulness	11/3-7	5/5	7/19	10/2	12/13	2/21	2:40–3:00 P.M.
46 ARIEL Perceiver and Revealer	11/8-12	5/6	7/20	10/3	12/14	2/22	3:00–3:20 P.M.
47 ASALIAH Contemplation	11/13-17	5/7	7/21	10/4	12/15	2/23	3:20–3:40 P.M.
48 MIHAEL Fertility, Fruitfulness	11/18-22	5/8	7/22	10/5	12/16	2/24	3:40–4:00 P.M.

7 NETZACH
Victory

Name of Angel—Primary Quality	Incarnation Angel Physical Birth and Life Purpose (Five-Day Period of Birth)	Heart Angel Qualities and Use of Emotions (Actual Birth Day)				Intellect Angel Qualities and Use of Intellect (Birth Time)
49 VEHUEL Elevation, Grandeur	11/23–27	5/9	7/23	10/6	12/17	2/25	4:00–4:20 P.M.
50 DANIEL Eloquence	11/28–12/2	5/10	7/24	10/7	12/18	2/26	4:20–4:40 P.M.
51 HAHASIAH Universal Medicine	12/3–7	5/11	7/25+26 A.M.	10/8	12/19	2/27	4:40–5:00 P.M.
52 IMAMIAH Expiation of Errors	12/8–12	5/12	7/26 P.M.+27	10/9	12/20	2/28+29	5:00–5:20 P.M.
53 NANAEL Spiritual Communication	12/13–16	5/13	7/28	10/10	12/21	3/1	5:20–5:40 P.M.
54 NITHAEL Rejuvenation and Eternal Youth	12/17–21	5/14	7/29	10/11	12/22	3/2	5:40–6:00 P.M.
55 MEBAHIAH Intellectual Lucidity	12/22–26	5/15	7/30	10/12	12/23	3/3	6:00–6:20 P.M.
56 POYEL Fortune and Support	12/27–31	5/16	7/31	10/13	12/24	3/4	6:20–6:40 P.M.

8 HOD
Glory, Splendor

Name of Angel—Primary Quality	Incarnation Angel: Physical Birth and Life Purpose (Five-Day Period of Birth)	Heart Angel: Qualities and Use of Emotions (Actual Birth Day)					Intellect Angel: Qualities and Use of Intellect (Birth Time)
57 NEMAMIAH Discernment	1/1–5	5/17	8/1	10/14	12/25	3/5	6:40–7:00 P.M.
58 YEIALEL Mental Force	1/6–10	5/18	8/2	10/15	12/26	3/6	7:00–7:20 P.M.
59 HARAHEL Intellectual Richness	1/11–15	5/19+20 A.M.	8/3	10/16	12/27 A.M.	3/7	7:20–7:40 P.M.
60 MITZRAEL Internal Reparation	1/16–20	5/20 P.M.+21	8/4	10/17	12/27 P.M.	3/8	7:40–8:00 P.M.
61 UMABEL Affinity and Friendship	1/21–25	5/22	8/5	10/18	12/28	3/9	8:00–8:20 P.M.
62 IAH–HEL Desire to Know	1/26–30	5/23	8/6	10/19	12/29	3/10	8:20–8:40 P.M.
63 ANAUEL Perception of Unity	1/31–2/4	5/24	8/7	10/20	12/30	3/11	8:40–9:00 P.M.
64 MEHIEL Vivification (Invigorate, Enliven)	2/5–9	5/25	8/8	10/21	12/31	3/12	9:00–9:20 P.M.